BUILDING SOCIAL CHANGE COMMUNITIES

To order additional copies of this book:
  Price: $2.80 each
         $2.25 for 10 or more copies
         $2.00 each for bookstores
Add 70¢ for the first book and 25¢ each additional book to cover postage and handling. Payment should accompany order. Make checks payable to:
  Movement for a New Society.

Philadelphia Movement for a New Society
4722 Baltimore Avenue
Philadelphia, PA 19143
  or
In the Southeast, from
Atlanta Movement for a New Society
P.O. Box 5434
Atlanta, GA 30307

Building Social Change Communities

The Training/Action Affinity Group Movement for a New Society

New, revised and enlarged edition.
Copyright ©1979, Movement for a New Society, Philadelphia, PA.
All rights reserved.

TABLE OF CONTENTS

1. **INTRODUCTION** 1
   Peter Woodrow and Susanne Terry

2. **FORMING A COMMUNAL HOUSEHOLD** 7
   Peter Woodrow

3. **NUTS AND BOLTS OF COMMUNAL LIVING** 15
   Berit Lakey

4. **THE CONSENSUS DECISION—MAKING PROCESS** 27
   Susanne Terry

5. **MEETING FACILITATION: THE NO-MAGIC METHOD** 35
   Berit Lakey

6. **RELATIONSHIPS IN COMMUNITY** 43
   Stephen Parker

7. **CREATIVE CONFLICT RESOLUTION** 57
   Christopher Moore

8. **SPINNING THE WEB: NETWORKS FOR SOCIAL CHANGE** 83
   Peter Woodrow

CHAPTER 1

INTRODUCTION

WHERE DID THIS BOOK COME FROM?

The Training/Action Affinity Group was a team of trainers for social change who lived at the Philadelphia Life Center and worked together offering training workshops for a variety of groups throughout the United States. We were a collective of the Movement for a New Society, a nation-wide network of social change groups. Among other things, we developed an expertise in the area of conflict resolution and used these skills to work with households and collectives in Philadelphia and with many social change groups in other areas of the country.

In February, 1976 The Affinity Group (Berit Lakey, Christopher Moore, Stephen Parker, Susanne Terry, and Peter Woodrow) ran a workshop on "Building Communities for Social Change." Five of the chapters of this book were originally written as a packet, and it was clear that a serious effort should be made to edit and expand the packet into a book that would be useful to the many groups of people across the country trying to pull together communities that focus on social change work. Over the past two years, Peter Woodrow has undertaken to edit the original chapters, write a few more, and collect some other writings by members of the Affinity Group. This revised, typeset and printed version is the result.

WHO IS THIS BOOK FOR?

This is a book for people looking for other people to work with and grow with in a long-term and committed effort to change the world we live in. It is not a book to help people form groups that focus all their energy on the maintenance of the members of those groups rather than being concerned about action in the world.

We hope that this book will be useful to people in many situations, not just those who live communally, want to live communally, or are already involved in growing networks of activists. We have tried to show that there is no single way to establish a "community for social change," but a great variety of models, some of which you yourself will invent to suit your situation.

SOME DEFINITIONS

What do we mean by "community" and by "social change"? By "community" we mean a commonly understood commitment between people to look out for each other; to come to each other's assistance in times of need (both personal and political); to think together about the way the world works and what needs to be done about it; and to insist with each other that we take decisive actions. Doing all this for each other consistently and well is difficult; working for significant change without it is even more difficult—and in the long term impossible. The political and economic institutions that we seek to change are powerful. We need all the strong and clear-eyed allies we can get. That is why we undertake to build this kind of community that helps us gain power ourselves.

You will notice that we did not say that "community" consists of a group of people living in a house or houses together or living on a farm in the country. These have been tried and they work. A large portion of this book is devoted to describing what we have learned about making that kind of *living situation* successful. But "community" is broader than that and is not limited to communal living. It can occur among workers in a factory, among neighbors, among individuals or families living in apartments or houses by themselves. Communal living can be convenient, economical, fun, and a good place to trap and eradicate personal habits of oppression such as sexism or ageism. But it is not the only way to achieve an effective social change community. In fact, living communally may at times be an inappropriate way to approach working for change in a particular locale or workplace.

"Social change" is a bit more elusive as a concept. All kinds of people, including the John Birch Society and the Progressive Labor Party, are for change in our society. For our purpose in this book we mean fundamental change of the political and economic institutions of society to achieve a just, humane, and egalitarian system. To do that effectively we need to eradicate any evidence of sexism, classism, racism, ageism, or any other ingrained in-humanism we find in ourselves and others. Working for social change means systematically dismantling these interlocking systems of oppression.

There are many brave and intelligent people already at work doing just that. The first task in building a political (social change) community is to find those people and build specific alliances with them. They will be there in the laundromat, the factory, at a local union meeting, around the corner, at the PTA—and some will be in the universities, churches, and traditional "movement" groups. There is no limit to the alliances we can make. If they are high quality alliances that include clear thinking, warmth, close friendships, commitment to each other, and effective action, then they begin to look like "communities for social change."

POLITICAL IMPLICATIONS OF COMMUNITY

In recent years there has been an increasing awareness among politically active people that our working style, living style and organizational structures have important political implications. The balance of this chapter will explore some of the implications of living and/or working in a political (social change) community.

1) Experimental models. As people engaged in the change process, political activists are constantly looking for new ways to do things (or reviving and adapting old ways). Political communities are an ideal place to experiment with new models. Our interactions in community have many dimensions—friendships, living together, giving each other encouragement and support, study and analysis, collective work, direct action and developing alternative institutions. Therefore we can try out many aspects of the "new society." In this way political communities have an advantage over organizations that engage only one aspect of our lives.

2) Alternatives to Competition. Modern North American society is based on the notion of competition—for jobs, security, material goods, school grades, love, and sex, among other things. Communities, of whatever form, provide an alternative based on sharing and cooperation. This is not a new notion, but an ancient one. In the years ahead, we may be faced with many occasions when our survival will depend on (re)developing cooperation. Community stands against the notion that competition is "just the way things are" and "nothing can be done about it." Competition is a practice fostered by an economic system that benefits a few. Part of the task of dismantling that economic system is whittling away at competitive outlooks and structures.

3) *Freeing Energy for Change Work.* In communities that include group living there are often substantial financial savings that result from sharing expenses for rent, food, etc. In the experience of MNS communities, this has freed time and energy for social change activities, since people can often meet their expenses with only part-time "bread labor." People can also agree to share child care or other responsibilities that then free time and energy.

4) *Work against "Isms."* Many of us are committed to working against the oppressive structures of our society such as sexism, classism, racism, and adultism (the unnecessary and oppressive wielding of power over children by adults). In order to do that work effectively we have to examine our own attitudes and the ways power is used in our lives. Are men assuming power over women, adults over children, middle and upper class people over people from working class backgrounds? Communities provide a place to identify the specific mechanisms of oppression in intimate detail and then work together to eliminate them. Once we understand how power works in our own lives we can discover ways to change the same mechanisms as they operate in the larger society.

5) *Organization.* The coming years may bring disruptions to American life. The energy crisis alone could seriously alter the ways we live. In some instances hardships will occur. People who are well organized—either in living communities or in close-knit and active networks—will be able to respond creatively to crises and disruption. A well-developed decision process, a history of successful cooperation, a sense of commitment to each other, clear long-range goals, and defined strategies for change will all aid social change communities to be among the most effective forces at times when other political movements flounder.

POWER AND COMMUNITY

Power is one of the issues that social change communities must face—particularly those with a commitment to nonviolence. Too often nonviolence has been confused with being "nice," gentle, or wishy-washy, rather than forceful and aggressive. To effect change we need to go about the systematic building of power. That means making allies—not only with people like ourselves, but with all kinds of people. It means living communities or networks of friends and allies become our bases for going powerfully into the world, *not* just safe havens where we can remain warm, close—and scared. Power is not built by focusing too much energy inward to the maintenance of the group of the individuals in it. The life of the group and the happiness of the people we call allies are crucial but cannot be our only preoccupation.

Many of us find power frightening. Too often it is used unjustly or rigidly—sometimes against us. We have seldom seen power wielded well. So the prospect of *us* having power and using it to change the world scares us. But without becoming powerful, movements for change will fail. Therefore one task facing social change communities is to encourage their members to face their feelings about power. Then we can go about building a broad power base, which can become one measure of our success.

We hope that people will use this book for ideas and encouragement, and find some jewels of wisdom from folks who have been trying to make social change communities work. Most of all, we hope your lives will be full of the joy and power that comes from taking responsibility for your world.

CHAPTER 2

FORMING A COMMUNAL HOUSEHOLD

Living communally has become almost commonplace in the United States both in rural and urban areas. People are getting better at it, more systematic, clearer about why they do it. For eight years people at the Philadelphia Life Center and elsewhere in the Movement for a New Society network have been experimenting with communal living, developing traditions and ways of operating that work well, based on experience. This chapter will lay out some of our folk wisdom in the hope that you can benefit from it as you put together new households or pick up the shards of an old one and add new people. Throughout this chapter, the assumption will be that the people forming households are interested in social change work—although many of the principles and practices described here could apply to any group of people looking for successful ways to share housing.

THE CRUCIAL FACTORS: GOALS, EXPECTATIONS, NEEDS AND LIFESTYLES

There are four crucial factors that must be clear in order for a communal household to function well: goals as a community, expectations of household members; individual needs and how/whether they get met; and group lifestyle.

Goals: Are you a cooperative (sharing a house in order to cut expenses), a communal household (sharing expenses, but also giving each other several kinds of personal and political support), a communal "family" (group with a longer-term commitment to each other and a wider range of interactions), or some unique blend of your own? Community goals refer to the broad strokes that describe what you are looking for in a group household. At times people with a particular interest form a household, and that central focus forms the basic goal. This is true of women's households, lesbian or gay households, religious/spiritual households and others. In these cases people are looking for a specific kind of support for an important part of their lives.

Goals for a household community can be also expressed in terms of time—how long people will stay with a house. Time has an important impact on how carefully people choose house members and how much energy members put into keeping relationships healthy.

Listed below are some examples of community goals. (This is not intended to be a complete list.)

The major goals of this communal household are to provide:
—Relatively inexpensive housing for people engaged in social change work.
—A living/support mechanism for social change activists.
—A relaxed, enjoyable group of people to live and have fun with.
—A "family" atmosphere that can nurture children.
—A spiritual household.
—A special support community for _____ (women, men, gays, lesbians, blacks, Jews, etc.).
—A stable community (in the midst of change) where people stay for at least _____ years.

Expectations: Every household has expectations of its members. Some of these are obvious, others are more subtle and maybe even unspoken. An example of an expectation that is often assumed and so is not mentioned at initial meetings with prospective members is the amount of time house members are expected to spend in the house. The eventual result of not clarifying this expectation goes something like this: "You're never home."

"Well, I'm busy."

"But you never have time for people in the house—it's like living with a stranger."

"I never said I would be here all the time."

"We assumed that if you were interested in living with people you would want to see them sometimes." Etc.

That is only one example of how an unclear expectation can work. Some expectations are hard to anticipate before you live together—many of them evolve over time. It is important, however, to establish at least a rough idea of expectations right from the start. The

FORMING A COMMUNAL HOUSEHOLD

following is a list of some common expectations of household members.

Each household member is expected to:
—Share in all household responsibilities (cooking, cleaning, buying, repairs, etc.).
—Share equally in household expenses (what about children?).
—Attend regular house meetings (how often?).
—Be involved with social change work (what kind?).
—Support other house members both politically and personally (by listening, helping solve problems, encouraging, etc.).
—Be at home for a minimum of _____ (meals, meetings, household play times).
—Attend household worship.
—Agree to take a chare of child care and nurture.
—Develop consciousness about sexism (ageism, other) and work against it.
—Bring conflicts to the surface and deal with them.
—Ask for what she/he needs from other house members.
—Pool all (part) income with other house members.

Needs: People come into a communal household with all kinds of needs and for many reasons. Most of these are fine and healthy, but some are suspect. Push, demand, cajole, do whatever you have to do, but find out what they are. Balanced by the expectations the household has of the group member are the expectations the group member has of the other members of the house. Everybody has needs of other people, and that is as it should be. In fact, you might well be suspicious of someone who claimed to have no needs. The point is only that there should be some kind of agreement as to which needs will be met by people in the household, and which will not.

We suggest as a part of the process of choosing people to live with that you take time to hear from each person what her/his needs are—all of them—and then which of those she/he expects to be met at least in part by the folks in the house. For example, Jane might say, "I need people in my household to care about me, to think with me from time to time about the directions of my life and social change work, to listen to me a reasonable amount of time, to play with me maybe once a week and to take on a portion of child care for my daughter. I will look outside the house for my needs for closer relationships, intimacy, for good friendships (although I do want to be friends with most of you in the house, too), and for ongoing political support (mainly from the people I work with)."

Lifestyle: Is this a vegetarian household? Are decor and furnishings a concern? How about neatness in the common areas of the house? How do members feel about smoking in the house? Do you want to feel free to walk around nude between your bedroom and the bathroom? Are you conscious about recycling and use of resources like water and gas?

Lifestyle is like the flavor or atmosphere of a house. Some of its aspects are intangible; others are quite specific and based on strongly (sometimes rigidly) held principles. There is a range of issues that partly define house lifestyle, which households have to deal with and sometimes set policies on. They are also the areas of greatest potential conflict among house members. Here is a partial list of lifestyle or policy issues:

Use of space
Use of common possessions
Decor in common areas
Neatness and cleanliness standards
Food—vegetarian/carnivore
Children
Pets
Smoking
Drugs and alcohol
Visitors
Sexual practices among house members (incest rule)
How decisions are made
Noise/quiet hours
Couples among singles
Conservation/recycling
Reverence for life (e.g. mice and rats)

More general principles: There are a number of other general guidelines that are important to keep in mind as you form a household.

1) What is in the open is discussable; what's not isn't. Don't assume anything. If you expect certain things from your housemates, tell them. If you see that a prospective house member has unrealistic expectations, ask about it, deal with it. Unmet needs, unclear goals or expectations and conflicts over lifestyle questions are the bane of communal households. Often these can be minimized or managed by getting any gripes or worries out in the open where they can be dealt with.

2) Don't live with someone you don't want to live with. This may seem obvious, but people agree with amazing regularity to live with people they *know* they will not get along with. Sometimes it is a matter of, "I want to live with Jack, and Jack and Harry are close friends and intend to live together. Harry drives me bonkers, but I'll put up with him in order to live in the same house with Jack." That is not fair to Jack, to Harry, or to yourself. Either find a way to live with Jack and not Harry, or don't live with either and find some other way to nurture your friendship with Jack. Of course you may have to compromise; just don't compromise away your own happiness and comfort with your living situation.

3) *Trust your own instincts.* Your feelings about a new household are important. If you are uneasy about something, don't choke it back for the sake of peace and quiet. What is a vague uneasiness now can become a major upset later. And don't be intimidated if you can't be specific. Trust your instincts enough to raise questions and to keep poking at yourself and others until the matter is clarified.

4) *Increasing size* requires greater organization and formality of agreements. A small group of four people can make decisions about living together and how to organize themselves in an informal manner. But in a group of six, seven and more, decisions must be more deliberate, agreements more formal (maybe even written down), and household organization more complex.

5) *Working together and living together* are not necessarily a good idea. We found out long ago that it is not necessary that you be able to live with the people you do political work with. In fact, sometimes it can be downright detrimental to either the work relationship, the housemate relationship, or both. It is best not to mix too many relationships with the same person. If you do, you have got to learn to be clear where one type of relationship ends and another begins.

FORMING OR REFORMING
A COMMUNAL HOUSEHOLD

Armed with the principles outlined above, how do you go about actually putting together a group of people to live together? It's not difficult—as clearly indicated by the thousands of households across the nation. But there are some ways you can go about forming a household community that may ensure greater success and longevity.

Getting a household together can be fun, instructive and empowering for the people involved. Communal households have been called a form of "intentional community." Part of that intentionality is reflected in the way people are cared about as decisions are made regarding membership in groups—a potentially hurtful experience. One of the ways to avoid hurting people unnecessarily is to announce from the start what your process will be for forming the household. Your process will depend largely on the type of household you are forming. The point is to *have* a process so that everyone involved knows what to expect.

First Step—Getting a Core Group: We recommend that the first step in pulling together a household be the formation of a small core group. If you have been living in a household of seven and three people have moved out, then you already have your core group. But if you are a new household and you know of fifteen people looking for housing, it is less clear how to proceed.

Our experience at the Life Center in Philadelphia has shown that getting together a new household can be a cumbersome, painful job that is often done under the pressure of time, landlords, and temporary living situations. In those circumstances people are not always thinking about each other and their plans as clearly as they might.

Often there is a pool of people looking for housing, some of whom know each other. The temptation, especially if you are all part of a social change network or a social gathering, is to get everyone together for a meeting to talk about setting up households. The difficulty with this move is that you have automatically created a group—even though it is a loose and informal one. In order to form households that will be smaller than this amorphous group, you will essentially have to exclude people. That feels like expelling them from a group that they were a part of. It is much easier and less painful for several people who know they want to live together to form a core group, look for a house to rent or buy, and decide the rough features of the house. Then, this core group can cleanly and simply add however many members they need to fill their household. In this way you will also steer clear of the tendency to agree to live with people you don't really want to live with in order to avoid hurting someone's feelings.

People have a lot of feelings about being included or excluded. It is very difficult to avoid triggering those feelings. The most important principles to follow are to keep communicating (on a one-to-one basis whenever possible) and to keep the proceedings open and honest. That may mean being courageous enough to tell someone quite directly that you don't want to live with them—and why. The "why" will probably have as much to do with you and your needs as them and their idiosyncrasies.

Next Steps: Assuming that you have formed a core group of three or four people, what other steps need to be taken to recruit additional members? We are presuming here a household that will be seven, eight, or more members. As we have noted above, when you are more than four or five people, your procedures and organizational structures need to be more formal. Otherwise, either people begin to feel like they don't have a say (because someone has taken over initiative/control), or disorganization reigns supreme (because no one has taken initiative). Look for processes that are fairly simple, that enable people to feel in charge and powerful, and get the job done. Here are some steps to consider:

1) Discuss goals, needs, expectations, and lifestyle questions among the group. Come to a tentative and rough idea about what your household will be like—what we might call a "household" profile. Don't fill in all the details; keep it flexible.
2) Decide *your* process for recruiting and accepting additional members—interviews, getting-to-know periods, trial living arrangements, how a decision will actually be made. For some suggestions and procedures, see the *Clearness* manual which is available through the Movement for a New Society, 4722 Baltimore Ave., Philadelphia, PA 19143.
3) Recruit potential members—on the basis of your tentative "household" profile.
4) Implement your decision process (2)—accept new members.
5) Agree to a revised household profile or contract. When you have your full house group, look at the tentative profile, revise it, add to it, write it up if you like. This forms what is essentially a household "contract." It should always be viewed as flexible and a growing thing—a statement of "where we are today." As you have house meetings, encounter conflicts and make new decisions, you will revise your group contract. If you have written down your original agreement, you may want to keep a written record of your decisions as you go along. Many houses just keep a notebook with minutes of house meetings.
6) Set a time to evaluate (a) how you are functioning as a group, and (b) how your "contract" or agreement is working. You

might set a trial period for the whole group that will require a specific time to make a decision to continue or not.

A word of warning: despite all the exhortations above to make things clear from the start—about goals, expectations, etc.—you will just have to let some things happen. A new group of people has to find its own way, decide by *doing* how they want to be with each other. As long as your basic trust and enjoyment of each other is alive and healthy you can greet your conflicts with a bit of relish and relax as your own group traditions grow around you. Have fun!

CHAPTER 3

SOME NUTS AND BOLTS OF COMMUNAL LIVING

Shall we rent or buy? Where do we begin to look for a house? How do we finance our communal house (or apartment)? These are some of the many questions to consider when forming a communal household. Very early on a group also needs to decide how information is shared and how decisions are made. And for those communities that will include children it is never too early to share individual feelings and thoughts about what it will mean to live with children. Careful thinking together in all these areas will avoid potential conflicts later (See Chapter 1.).

BUY OR RENT?

Pro renting: easier to deal with for groups where
   a. People don't have a long range commitment to the group or to the geographical location (students, people in transition, engaged in short term projects).
   b. People who have no previous experience with communal living, people who are still hurting from and reacting to a negative experience, or people who want to try communal life for a given period of time.
   c. You cannot raise money for a down payment on a house or cannot get a mortgage (because of uncertain job situations, etc.).

Pro buying:
   a. It is usually cheaper in the long run.
   b. It provides more of a sense of permanence and thus
      —More willingness on the part of members to work out conflicts,
      —A better connection with the neighborhood.
   c. More freedom to make changes in the house.

d. More stakes in the looks of the place.
   e. A chance to experiment with collective ownership of property.

Sometimes you cannot find the right house to buy in the right neighborhood and may settle for renting while you keep looking.

WHERE?

For people who work for social change the question of where to live is a political one as well as an economic one. When considering the neighborhood these are some of the factors to look at:
   —What are some of the economic and class structures of the neighborhood? Who do you want to identify with and work with?
   —Is the neighborhood racially mixed? If not, why? Can you be who you want to be and do what you want to do in a non-integrated neighborhood?
   —Are there houses available that are both roomy enough for communal households and reasonable in price?
   —Is your lifestyle/politics likely to produce such antagonism in the neighborhood that an excessive amount of energy will go into surviving? Are there sources of support?
   —Is it within reasonable distance of jobs and other people that you want to continue (or start) to relate to?

HOW TO FIND HOUSING

In most places realtors have the best information on what is available. There are people who do not want to put up a "For Sale" sign outside their house or advertise for fear of intruders (or because of racial prejudice). Realtors will arrange for you to inspect properties that are for sale or rent and will help with details in transfer of ownership/occupancy. It is probably best to be open about the fact that you are looking for a house that will be suitable for communal use. In many places there are zoning regulations that are designed to keep communes out. The attitude of the realtor is likely to give you a clue as to whether you are going to run into zoning problems.

Advertising for what you want and reading classified ads may also provide good leads. Personal contacts, asking people in the neighborhood if they know of housing that will soon become available, are additional possibilities. Old people are sometimes left in houses that are much too big for them and would like to move to an apartment, a retirement home or to relatives, but do not have the energy to go through the ordeal of selling and moving. We have known old people who were glad to sell to a communal group that was considerate and willing to do a lot of the actual legwork in the transfer of ownership and in the moving of belongings.

FINANCING

Unless you have available capital to pay cash, you will need a mortgage. Before asking a bank for a mortgage (which may not give you one anyway because your house is in the wrong neighborhood or because you don't have a "reliable" source of income), explore sources of money among your friends, churches, and organizations. Some people are glad to invest in enterprises they believe in rather than to let the bank do the investing for them. If you are an explicit social change community you may explore the possibility of a mortgage with low or no interest from a sympathetic party. This is one way movement people with access to money can be helpful to the movement.

Whatever the source of financing you use, be sure that arrangements about security of the loan, repayment, etc. are clear and legal. If you don't use a realtor, it might be wise to consult a friendly lawyer who would be willing to tell you what needs doing (or who will make the arrangements for you—probably for a fee).

OWNERSHIP

The ownership of a communal house may be a very important factor in the way a group of people relate to it, because the way decisions are made about the house is often affected by the fact that a particular person (or persons) actually own the property.

Here are some possible ways of owning a house:

1) Non-profit corporation: The group that lives together forms a non-profit corporation and owns the house as a group. It is possible to set up a corporation without the use of a lawyer, but do investigate carefully the laws in your state. If individual members of the corporation put money into the acquisition of the house, it would be considered a loan to the corporation like any other loan. Be clear about interest, repayment, etc. Also, decide on how many people become members of the corporation as well as how they leave the corporation.

2) Personal ownership: The house could be owned by an individual or a couple. This is often the case when a communal household is formed by adding people to an already existing household. In order to avoid friction regarding the use and upkeep of the house it is important to spell out rights and responsibilities very early. We have found it preferable to work out an agreement concerning finances of the house (upkeep, possible future sale, etc.) where decisions can be made communally rather than by the party who holds title to the property (e.g. people who have lived in the house a certain time will be able to share in the profit/loss if the house is sold according to the share or rent they have paid).

3) Partnership: The house could be owned by a partnership of the people who live there (different from a corporation by personal responsiblity for liabilities)—check local laws.

4) Land Trust: If the property were held in a land trust there would be no question of selling just because the group broke up. For information about land trusts, turn to *The Community Land Trust: A New Model for Land Tenure in America,* International Independence Institute, West Road, Box 183, Ashby, MA 01431.

HOUSE/COMMUNITY MEETINGS★

For groups that want to function in an egalitarian way, it is crucial to develop structures that encourage collective decision making.

★NOTE: The processes needed to keep any intentional community healthy are very similar whether or not the people live in the same house. For ease of expression I shall refer mostly to house meetings.

"Letting things happen spontaneously" or "letting people do their thing" is likely to produce little personal growth and to continue social patterns of sexism, ageism, and elitism.

In regular meetings (before as well as after the formation of a community) a group can:

1) Develop a sense of corporateness. A group can be more than the sum of its members, but only if the sense of wholeness is allowed to emerge as people think and act together.

2) Work out common goals and understandings. It is not safe to assume that a group of people see things the same way and that they are indeed working toward the same goals. To rely on the statements of a few outspoken members does not work either; everybody needs the opportunity to be heard and support to express his or her opinion.

3) Solving problems. In any group that lives or works (or even just plays) together, problems will arise. If they are not dealt with adequately on the basis of common goals and understandings, the problems tend to develop into conflicts between members. Unless the group meets with regularity and expects to solve problems together, minor issues may grow to crisis proportions before some people feel that they *have* to do something. The "too little, too late" syndrome can be avoided by regular house meetings.

4) Decide together what needs doing, when and how. If common needs (housecleaning, repairs, projects) are not discussed and decided on by everybody involved, factions and resentments are bound to crop up. Decisions need to be made by the whole group, especially if one of the goals is fairly equal sharing of tasks and responsibilities.

It is entirely reasonable to make membership in a house (or other close community) contingent on willingness to attend regular meetings.

For a group to grow in depth as well as in efficient functioning, time needs to be set aside for sharing of personal experiences and ideas as well as "business." Some groups find it useful to deal with these different agendas at different times. Other groups include some of each whenever they meet. It is important to recognize, however, that "business" meetings get more bearable if participants have a chance to touch base with each other as people, and that sharing in depth takes time.

BUSINESS MEETINGS

For specific suggestions on how to have good and efficient meetings I refer to my paper, "Meeting Facilitation, the No Magic Method." Generally, in our experience, it has been useful to include some standard components:

1) Choose a facilitator or facilitators. This person(s) will have the responsibility to think about *the group* rather than thinking of his or her own point of view, and to move things along, making sure clear decisions are made, etc.

2) Form an agenda so that everybody knows what needs to be covered. It is best to think about the agenda beforehand (good flow, people's attention span, possible snags, etc.). This is possible if the facilitator is chosen before the meeting and collects agenda items from others.

3) Agree on ending time. It is easier to have a discussion that is to the point when people have contracted with each other about the times they are prepared to spend together. This way individuals can also budget their energy in such a way that their attention span extends to the end of the meeting.

4) Begin with something that brings people together—singing, silence, excitement sharing (something good, exciting, fun that has happened to you lately).

5) "Hypes and gripes"—A useful exercise where people for the first five minutes are encouraged to say only things that have pleased them about the house in the past week (the "hypes" part), and then for another five minutes only those things that have bothered or irritated them (in the "gripes" part). During a gripe session people are encouraged to state their gripes without qualifying or explaining them away, and no response is allowed until after the time is up. We have found this to be a reasonably low-key way to surface small problems before they grow into big ones. Also, most of us need encouragement to look for the good things and then to express appreciation, as well as to dare to offend or hurt somebody by stating our own dislikes.

6) *Evaluation.* By thinking quickly back over the meeting, sorting out what went well and what needs improvement, a group can learn how to have better and better meetings. A routine evaluation should only take a few minutes.

SHARING MEETINGS

In addition to knitting the group closer together and providing a basis for developing common goals and expectations, the house meeting can play an important role in the personal growth of the participants. It is a place where one's situation can be reflected upon, where feedback and support for change can be requested and given. There are a variety of ways to start sharing who we are and where we are coming from, such as looking at lifelines (important developments from stage to stage of one's life), turning points, people who were important for us, ideas that influenced us, forces that acted upon us, etc. It is important to remember to set aside a certain amount of time—adequate, but not more than people are able or willing to give. If several people are going to share about themselves, make sure that they have roughly the same amount of time. If certain topics bring tears, it is helpful if the listeners pay warm and close attention rather than either to ignore the tears or try to stop them. Real people have real feelings; the stiff upper lip is hopefully a thing of the past. At the end of the time for sharing pay close atrtention to how the people involved are feeling—it can be unsettling to share deeply of one's life. Forming a close circle, silence, group back rubs, etc., will communicate appreciation for the person(s) who opened her/himself to the others as well as to give some space to shift gears.

HOUSE/COMMUNITY RETREATS

Most groups could use an occasional retreat, or time away from home together. At special times (when under stress, after a project, after the loss of a member, before times of being away from each other) a retreat can be invaluable. Being away from day-to-day surroundings helps people see each other in a new light and have a different experience of each other. The connected time without other claims on people's attention can help deepen knowledge of each other and contribute to a sense of belonging together. A retreat can be anywhere—from somebody else's house down the street to camping in the woods (even at home, if need be). It can be used to play, reflect, discuss, analyze, build visions, etc. Some preplanning usually pays off—both in terms of logistics and food, as well as activities—unless the purpose specifically is to be spontaneous and playful.

MEN'S AND WOMEN'S GROUPS

Increasingly, houses and other communities are finding it helpful to break into separate women's and men's groups. These groups may serve several purposes:
—To provide safety and support when dealing with issues of sex role oppression or other emotionally loaded subjects.
—To think through issues and strategies, to ensure that everyone can participate and that ideas can surface and be developed in a less competitive atmosphere.
—To give mutual support for personal growth.

Separate groups may happen only occasionally for specific purposes or may be built into the regular house process.

ORGANIZATION OF COMMON TASKS

If a group wants to operate efficiently and in a spirit of equality it is crucial that structures be developed for sharing common tasks. If tasks are left to whomever feels like doing them or has the time, a situation of inequality will persist with enormous potential for open conflict, blatant sexism, and little growth for the individuals involved.

Each house will need to find structures that suit its own needs, but some general guidelines can be suggested:
1) *List the tasks* that need to be done to maintain the community.
2) *Sort them out* into tasks that need to be done frequently (like cooking dinner) and those that can be done less often (such as cleaning the living room or repairing leaky faucets).
3) *Divide the jobs* into roughly equal chunks according to the number of people involved.

Most of the communal houses we know have found it useful to treat cooking separately from other house chores, which are often assigned on a monthly basis. The weekly house meeting serves as a time for working out cooking schedules and rotating other tasks. Some people find it easier to get their work done if they work in pairs or small groups. Others do fine by themselves; still others prefer a time when all the house members participate in a housecleaning "blitz" together.

Specially scheduled house workdays are helpful for doing repairs and improvements that do not fall under the heading "chores." Working together on common projects may serve a community building function as well.

Houses sometimes find that they have members who are regularly too busy to get their share of the housework done or who don't even sign up because they have such a lot of more "important" things to do. Such people might be questioned about why they are in community. When others frequently have to pick up the work or live in a neglected environment, it seems legitimate to raise the question of exploitation.

SKILL SHARING

If it appears that the same people do the same jobs over and over again, it would be wise to set up conscious ways of learning from each other. A community where everybody has basic maintenance skills (food preparation, cleaning, simple carpentry and plumbing, meeting facilitation) is likely to endure and to be a place where equality is more than a platitude.

MONEY

Money, like sex and children, has the great potential to create tension and discord in a house. In our society so many symbols and feelings are attached to questions of money that it is best never to assume that everybody has the same attitude and always to proceed with caution.

Some communal houses practice complete income sharing, while others are content with expense sharing. Some groups that are aspiring to income sharing have found it helpful to do it by degrees. They might start out by pooling a certain percentage of their income and gradually increasing the percentage. Expense sharing is probably more common. Here the members of the house share equally (or however they determine) the common expenses, but retain control over the rest of their incomes. In considering how to deal with money it is important to find out what the individuals involved are ready for. Total income sharing obviously raises a lot more possibilities for disagreement that expense sharing. Looking at childhood experiences related to money and economic status can be helpful both in understanding where disagreements come from, and in putting a social change perspective on our own attitudes towards money.

CHILDREN

A book could be written about children and their care and participation in communities. We do not claim to have any definitive answers, but on the basis of our own experience, we venture the following:

1) Children deserve attention and care from all the people they live with. People who do not like to be around children or who consider time spent with them a waste of time, should not live in a house with children.

2) Most communal households realize and respect the special relationship between parents and children, but do assume that a certain responsibilities for the care of children will be shared by all the adults. Clearly spelling out mutual expectations between parents and the other house members regarding the amount and nature of time spent in childcare can prevent misunderstandings, disappointments, and resentments.

3) Providing a regular space in house meetings for considering the children gives all the people who are involved with the children a chance to share information, concerns, insights and questions and will provide a forum for solving problems as they arise.

4) Becoming conscious of ways we were brought up ourselves and sharing this information with other house members will help anchor discussions about child rearing theories in our own experiences and thus be closer to real life. It will also help house members understand each other's reactions to children.

5) In order to deal creatively with the tribulations that are inevitable in living with children, it is important to remind each other of happy times with them. Sharing our observations of growth and achievements in individual children is as necessary as thinking together about how to get over rough spots. Encouraging each other, both adults and children, when we notice creative responses in particular situations, helps to foster a climate of growth for everybody.

6) When a non-parent is doing childcare it is important that the parents let the children know who is in charge so that adults will not be played off against each other. It is often easier for children and new adults in their lives to work on their relationships if the parents remove themselves from the situation.

7) In conflicts about childrearing in a communal household, it may be especially wise to use an outside facilitator or at least someone who is not a party to the conflict.

Children are sometimes maddening, sometimes rewarding, but at all times a new challenge to our visions for the future and our strategies for building a new society.

CHAPTER 4

THE CONSENSUS DECISION-MAKING PROCESS

This chapter is an introduction to the process of making decisions by consensus. It covers a working definition of consensus, when consensus can be used, what it is not, the tone and atmosphere that are most conducive to using consensus, the conditions necessary for using the consensus process, and a few questions that arise about the use of consensus. Since consensus decision-making is best learned by practice, this paper in no way attempts to cover all possibilities or questions that come up.

WAYS THAT GROUPS CAN MAKE DECISIONS

1) voting—decisions are made according to the wishes of a majority or fixed percentage of members.

2) fiat—a decree, sanction, or order is given from a person or persons in authority.

3) delegated authority—a group assigns a person or persons to make a specific decision or set of decisions for the group (this obviously does not say how the small group makes the decision, but only that the larger group waives the right to make the decision and trusts the smaller group).

4) decision by non-decision—an often tried method in groups dealing with an issue that is too hot to handle, gets tabled or filibustered; or used when the group cannot seem to find a process to discuss the issue reasonably and bring it to conclusion.

5) consensus—a process through which an entire group seeks out the best decision to which all can agree.

In the consensus process:
a) An issue is brought to a group, usually in the form of a proposal.
b) The issue is discussed and questioned, and concerns raised.
c) Differences and disagreements as well as similarities are drawn out and encouraged.
d) Modifications and adaptations of the original proposal are made.
e) The group creates a new proposal based on ideas raised in discussion.
f) The group reaches a decision that is acceptable to all in spite of reservations or differences.

Consensus is *not* unanimity. It is not necessary for every person in the group to feel that this is the solution that they would most want, or even think is best; members may feel, however, that this is the best solution that can be reached at this time and under these circumstances.

WHEN CAN YOU USE CONSENSUS?

Consensus can be used effectively only when there is common agreement to find solutions acceptable to the entire group. This occurs most often when it is a feeling of the group that no decision is more important than the group itself—that is, when the ongoing life of the group is important, or solidarity and a sense of well-being among group members is a priority, consensus is more likely to be an effective method of decision-making.

THE ATMOSPHERE THAT HELPS IN USING CONSENSUS

1) It is important that there be an atmosphere in which people's intelligence and thinking are affirmed. Groups members must be confident that they will be heard and their ideas respected.

2) There should be the willingness to bring out, listen to, and deal with hidden feelings that are affecting people's willingness or ability to hear ideas and make decisions.

3) For a group to use consensus successfully, it must understand the necessity of surfacing and sensitively dealing with grudges and conflicts that are affecting the group.

4) For a group to operate at its full potential and make its best decisions, power relationships must be continuously pointed out and examined carefully. It is no longer appropriate for decisions to be influenced by people simply because they are older, stronger, more wealthy, male, or louder.

5) It is necessary to have the expectation that the best decisions reflect the thinking and agreement of all members.

BUT MY GROUP DOESN'T HAVE THAT ATMOSPHERE!

Obviously, if you delay until your group reaches perfection in any or all of these points, you may have a bit of wait! That's not what is meant. Look at your group: do you see it moving toward the kind of atmosphere stated here? If so, you are probably close to or ready to try consensus. If not, perhaps this will help point out to you those ways in which you can start building the kind of community within your group that will help your decision-making.

CONDITIONS FOR USE OF CONSENSUS

1) The group needs to understand the process and agree to it.

2) There needs to be a facilitator, clerk, or chairperson with both flexibility and firmness.

3) The group should have a fairly high degree of homogeneity or bonding philosophy.

4) People in the group should have some commitment to the on-goingness of the group rather than just to their own personal agendas.

5) There needs to be a general assumption that everyone has something valuable to say.

WHY USE CONSENSUS?

And if those conditions exist, what then is the advantage of using consensus? More importantly, what is the advantage to helping move your group to the point where it can use consensus? Here are some arguments for use of the consensus process:

1) It decides without voting, and therefore without a "losing" and a "winning" side. Consensus makes a stronger decision than voting—everyone can give willing assent to an idea and participate more fully in implementation.

2) It is a way of accumulating viewpoints and synthesizing, rather than choosing one idea over another.

3) It aims at persuasion and not coercion.

4) It provides an opportunity for everyone to contribute information and participate. (You don't have to be an expert at Roberts' Rules of Order to take part!)

5) There are more opinions than in a voting system.

6) People get a chance to hash things over and as a result develop a better proposal than if a quick vote had been taken.

7) Consensus affirms that the integrity of the group is more important than any one issue that the group may face.

8) It affirms the group's ability to think as a group rather than considering proposals from individuals and then compromising.

9) Consensus discourages back room politics and encourages openness.

PARLIAMENTARY PROCEDURE

The consensus process is based on common sense rather than parliamentary procedure. Roberts' Rules of Order and consensus decision-making do not go hand in hand. If your group is now using Roberts' Rules and you wish to use consensus, you must be flexible and modify and adapt rules of procedure.

The more effective method of using consensus, however, is the using of the group facilitation process described in Berit Lakey's paper *Meeting Facilitation: The No Magic Method* (see Chapter 5). This functional and down-to-earth process is free of the regimentation of rules that are often incomprehensible to those bound by them.

A word of caution: the absence of Roberts' Rules does not mean that anything goes! Consensus process is not based on letting anyone do or say anything she or he wants. It is based on an orderly progression and thoughtful discussion of ideas.

The questions that good facilitators always are asking themselves are:
a) What is happening to the people in this group?
b) Are people following and understanding what is going on?
c) What is the most reasonable next step that people will understand?

WHAT DOES CONSENSUS LOOK LIKE IN PRACTICE?

One example might look like this (remember there are dozens of scenarios for how proposals can get made, discussed, and decisions made):

A proposal comes before a group. The facilitator asks for clarifying questions *only*. As soon as the questions start drifting into the category of "What if such and such would happen...?" then the facilitator indicates to the group that they seem to be moving into raising concerns. She/he then asks the group to brainstorm concerns (recorded on large chart). Also brainstorm positives about the proposal. Next people might meet in small groups to do preliminary thinking and discussion about the proposal and concerns. Each small group sees what it can agree to and records it. The group then briefly report back what they have tentatively decided. It might sound something like this:

"Group One thinks that the proposal is excellent but feels that the date is an unrealistic one. We would suggest a later time."

"Group Two agrees with the proposal in principle but would like a later date, and we have real reservations about how the people would be selected."

As the reports are in, the facilitator(s) (use more than one when possible) makes an educated guess at what the group is thinking and summarizes, "It sounds as if we can agree to the proposal tentatively if we can work out the following points: date (and it seems that everyone would like a later one); personnel and the way they are chosen; and a way to follow up..."

People might make suggestions from the floor to solve the problems, or the small groups can meet again to do that work.

Two points that make this process go smoothly are the facilitator's ability to sense and state points of agreement and to encourage an orderly flow of ideas and concerns without letting the group go off on tangents.

WHAT IF?

1) *What if one or two people disagree with the rest of the group?*
   Make sure their ideas have been listened to carefully. If it seems that the rest of the group has considered their ideas but there is still disagreement, ask if the one or two feel strongly enough to block consensus. They may stand aside if they feel that the group has acknowledged their ideas. Sometimes people are willing to stand aside if special considerations can be made such as:
   a) They don't have to do the work on a given task.
   b) If their dissenting ideas are recorded.
   c) If it is stipulated that the decision does not set precedent and therefore cannot be used as basis for future decisions.
   d) A trial period set for testing the decision and its implementation (this would include a time for evaluation and re-negotiation if necessary).

2) *What if the group is evenly divided?*
   Ask people to meet in small groups to develop a proposal that they think *everyone can agree to*. Or call for silence so people can think and reflect.

3) *What if there seems to be pressure exerted on one or two persons to*

"give in"?
It is the responsibility of the facilitator to insure that the individual's right to disagree is protected. The facilitator has several options for doing this depending upon the situation:
   a) State again for the person(s) what the facilitator senses the agreement among the rest of the group to be. She/he then asks the one or two persons who are disagreeing to state their specific objections. This is often helpful if there have been misunderstandings on either part.
   b) If the objections seem to be reasonable, the facilitator can ask the group to meet again in small groups to consider the person's ideas. The group may also continue to meet as a whole, but unnecessary pressure is often relieved by small group work.
   c) If the objections seem to be inappropriate or off the track, the facilitator can state as objectively as possible that it is her/his sense that the group has listened as well as it can, but the person's concerns are not appropriate for this time.
   d) Call for a break to defer the decision, if possible—i.e., give breathing and thinking space to dissenters. This could be as little as five minutes or as much as hours or days.

4) *What if the group cannot reach agreement?*
The facilitator or a group member restates clearly where the group has gone in its discussion, what the outstanding issues are, what steps might next be taken, and where the decision-making can begin at the next meeting.

WHEN A DECISION IS MADE

Double check to make sure there is agreement to a specific and restated decision. The facilitator might say, "I would like to check again—it is my understanding that we reached agreement that we will meet on alternate Tuesdays at 7 PM in Room 600. The exception to that will be next Tuesday when we will meet at 7:30. Is that agreed?"

When the agreement on any issue is made, clarify details and get agreement on implementation. Congratulate yourselves—literally. Shake hands, applaud, or take a deep breath. But do acknowledge that you have done it!

A FINAL WORD

Consensus is not easier than voting. In many ways it requires much more thought and energy. However, it is not necessarily a bulky or time consuming process. Consensus decisions can be made quite efficiently once a group is used to working with the process. Remember, it takes time for a group to work together well.

CHAPTER 5

MEETING FACILITATION: THE NO MAGIC METHOD

Meetings are occasions when people come together to get something done, whether it is sharing information or making decisions. They may be good, bad or indifferent. Some of the ingredients of good meetings are:
—Commonly understood goals.
—A clear process for reaching those goals.
—An awareness that people come with their personal preoccupations and feelings as well as an interest in the subject at hand.
—A sense of involvement and empowerment; people feeling that the decisions are *their* decisions; that they are able to do what needs doing.

While there is no foolproof way to insure successful meetings, there are a number of guidelines that will go a long way toward helping groups to meet both joyfully and productively. Most people can learn how to facilitate a good meeting, but it does take some time and attention. The more people within a group who are aware of good group process skills, the easier the task of the facilitator and the more satisfactory the meeting.

A facilitator is not quite the same as a leader or chairperson, but more like a clerk in a Quaker meeting. A facilitator accepts responsibility to help the group accomplish a common task: to move through the agenda in the time available and to make necessary decisions and plans for implementation.

A facilitator makes no decisions for the group, but suggests ways that will help the group move forward. He or she works in such a way that the people present at the meeting are aware that *they* are in charge, that it is *their* business that is being conducted, and that each person has a role to play.

It is important to emphasize that the responsibility of the facilitator is to *the group* and its work rather than to the individuals within the group. Furthermore, a person with a high stake in the issues discussed will have a more difficult task functioning as a good facilitator.

If at all possible, plan the agenda before the meeting. It is easier to modify it later than to start from scratch at the beginning of the meeting. If very few agenda items are known before the meeting starts, try to anticipate by thinking about the people who will be there and what kind of process will be helpful to them.

In the agenda include:

1) Something to gather people, to bring their thoughts to the present, to make them recognize each other's presence (singing, silence, brief mention of good things that have happened to people lately, etc.).

2) Agenda review—it's a good idea to have the agenda writen on large sheets of newsprint or on a blackboard, so that everybody can see it. By reviewing the agenda the facilitator can give the participants a chance to modify the proposed agenda and then to contract to carry it out.

3) Main items—if more than one item needs to be dealt with it is important to set priorities:
  a. *If at all possible, start with something that can be dealt with reasonably easily.* This will give the group a sense of accomplishment and energy.
  b. *The more difficult or lengthier items, or those of most pressing importance,* come next. If there are several, plan to have quick breaks between them to restore energy and attention (just a stretch in place, a rousing song, a quick game).
  c. *A big item may be broken into several issues* and discussed one at a time to make it more manageable. Or it may be helpful to suggest a process of presenting the item with background information and clarification, breaking into small groups for idea sharing and making priorities, and then returning to the main group for discussion.
  d. *Finish with something short and easy* to provide a sense of hope for next time.

4) Announcements

5) *Evaluation*—serves several purposes: to provide a quick opportunity for people to express their feelings about the proceedings and thus to provide a sense of closure to the experience; and to learn to have better meetings in the future.

Estimate the time needed for each item and put it on the agenda chart. This will:
—Indicate to participants the relative weights of the items.
—Help participants tailor their participation to the time available.
—Give a sense of the progress of the meeting.

The tone of a meeting is usually set in the beginning. It's important to start on a note of confidence and energy and with the recognition that those present are people, not just roles and functions. Sometimes singing will do this—especially in large gatherings—or a quick sharing of good things which have happened to individual people lately. The time it takes is repaid by the contribution it makes to a relaxed and upbeat atmosphere in which participants are encouraged to be real with each other.

AGENDA REVIEW

1) Go through the whole agenda in headline form, giving a brief idea of what is to be covered and how.
3) Then, and not before, ask for questions and comments.
4) Don't be defensive about the agenda you have proposed, but don't change everything at the suggestion of one person—check it out with the group first.
5) If major additions are proposed, make the group aware that adjustments must be made because of limited time available, like taking something out, postponing something until later, etc.
6) If an item that some people do not want to deal with is suggested for discussion, consider that there is no consensus and it cannot be included at that time.
7) Remember that your responsibility as facilitator is to the whole group and not to each individual.
8) When the agenda has been amended, ask the participants if they are willing to accept it—and insist on a response. They

need to be aware of having made a contract with you about how to proceed. Besides, it is their meeting!

AGENDA ITEMS PROPER

1) *Arrange (before the meeting) to have somebody else present* each item.
2) *Encourage the expression of various viewpoints*—the more important the decision, the more important it is to have all pertinent information (facts, feelings and opinions) on the table.
3) *Expect differences of opinion*—when handled well, they can contribute greatly to creative solutions.
4) *Be suspicious of agreements reached too easily*—test to be sure that people really do agree on essential points.
5) *Don't let discussion continue between two people,* but ask for comments by others. After all, it is the group that needs to make decisions and carry them out.
6) *As much as possible, hold people to speaking for themselves only* and to being specific when they refer to others. NO "some people say...," "we all know," "they would not listen..." Even though this practice is scary in the beginning, it will foster building of trust in the long run.
7) *Keep looking for minor points of agreement* and state them—it helps morale.
8) *Encourage people to think of fresh solutions* as well as to look for possible compromises.
9) *In tense situations* or when solutions are hard to reach, remember humor, affirmation, quick games for energy, change of places, small buzz groups, silence, etc.
10) *When you test for consensus,* state in question form everything that you feel participants agree on. Be specific: "Do we agree that we'll meet on Tuesday evenings for the next two months and that a facilitator will be found at each meeting to function at the next one?" Do *not* merely refer to a previous statement: "Do you all agree that we should do it the way it was just suggested?"
11) *Insist on a response.* Here again the participants need to be conscious of making a contract with each other.
12) *If you find yourself drawn into the discussion in support of a particular position,* it wold be preferable to step aside as facilitator until the next agenda item. This can be arranged beforehand if you anticipate a conflict of interest.

13) *Almost any meeting will benefit from quick breaks* in the proceedings—energy injections—provided by short games, songs, a common stretch, etc.

EVALUATION

In small meetings (up to 50 people at least) it is often wise to evaluate how things went (the meeting process, that is, not the content). A simple format: on top of a large sheet of newsprint or a blackboard put a plus sign on the left side, a minus sign in the middle, and an arrow pointing ahead on the right side. Under the plus sign list positive comments, things that people felt good about. Under the minus sign, list things that could have been done better, that did not come off so well. Under the arrow, list specific suggestions for how things could have been improved.

Don't get into arguments about whether something was in fact helpful or not; people have a right to their feelings. It is not necessary to end with a positive comment. Meetings almost invariably get better after people get used to evaluating how they function together.

CLOSING

Try to end the meeting in the same way it was started—with a sense of gathering. Don't let it just fizzle. A song, some silence, standing in a circle, shaking hands—anything that affirms the groups as such and puts a feeling of closure on the time spent together is good.

SPECIAL ROLES

"VIBES WATCHER"

At times when the discussion is expected to be particularly controversial or when there are more people than the facilitator can be awarely attentive to, it may make more sense to appoint a "vibes watcher"—a person who will pay atention to the emotional climate and energy level of the attenders. Such a person is encouraged to interrupt the proceedings when necessary with an observation of how things are going and to suggest remedies when there is a problem.

As "vibes watcher" you pay most attention to the nonverbal communication, such as:
1) *Body language:* are people yawning, dozing, sagging, fidgeting, leaving?
2) *Facial expressions:* are people alert or "not there", looking upset, staring off into space?
3) *Side conversations:* are they distracting to the facilitator or to the group?
4) *People interrupting* each other.

It is often difficult to interpret such behavior correctly. Therefore it may be wise to report what you observed and possibly suggest something to do about it. If energy is low a quick game, stretch, or a rousing song may wake people up. If tension or conflict level is preventing people from hearing each other, a simple getting up and finding new places to sit may help. A period of silence might also be helpful when people may have a chance to relax a bit and look for new insights.

It is important for the vibes watcher to keep a light touch—don't make people feel guilty or defensive. Also, be confident in your role—there is no reason for apologizing when you have an observation or a suggestion for the group—you are doing them a favor.

PROCESS OBSERVER

From time to time any group can benefit from having somebody observe how it works. During periods of conflict or transition (changing consciousness about sexism, for example) a process observer may be of special value.

While functioning as a process observer be careful not to get involved in the task of the group. A notepad for short notations will help you to be accurate. Remember to notice helpful suggestions or procedures that have moved the group forward. Once a group has a sense of its strengths it is easier to consider the need for improvements.

Here are some specific things you might look for:
1) What was the general atmosphere in which the group worked? relaxed? tense?
2) How were the decisions made?
3) If there was any conflict, how was it handled?
4) Did everybody participate? Were there procedures which encouraged participation?
5) How well did the group members listen to each other?
6) Were there recognized leaders within the group?
7) How did the group interact with the facilitator?
8) Were there differences between male and female participation?

When you as a process observer (whether appointed or not) are paying specific attention to patterns of participation, an easy device would be to keep score on paper. In a small group a mark can be made next to a person's name every time she/he speaks. If you are looking for difference in participation patterns between categories of people, such as male/female, black/white, new member/old member, etc., keeping track of number of contributions in each category is enough.

In giving feedback to the group, try to be matter of fact and specific so that people do not get defensive and can know exactly what you are talking about. Again, remember to mention the strengths you observed in the group.

If you take it upon yourself to function as a process observer without checking with the group beforehand, be prepared for some hostility. Your contribution may turn out to be very valuable, but a lot of tact and sensitivity is called for.

CO-FACILITATOR

Instead of the usual practice of having one facilitator it is often wise to have two facilitators. Here are some of the reasons and circumstances for team facilitation:
1) More information and ideas are available during the planning.
2) More energy (physical and emotional) is available to the group—especially during times of conflict or when handling complicated matters.
3) If a facilitator becomes personally involved in the discussion, it

is easy to hand the job over to the co-facilitator for the time being.
4) Co-facilitation is a way for more people to gain experience and become skilled facilitators.
5) It is less exhausting, demanding, and scary.

For people who are not used to working as a team, it is probably wise to divide responsibility for the agenda clearly before the meeting. However, co-facilitation means that the person who is not currently "on duty" is still responsible for paying attention as "vibes watcher" and pitching in to help clarify issues, test for consensus, etc.

In evaluating their work together, people who work as co-facilitators can help each other by giving feedback and support, and thus learn to grow.

CHAPTER 6

RELATIONSHIPS IN COMMUNITY

The success of social change communities requires building new healthy kinds of relationships between people. We are still in the early stages of learning what those relationships might look like. The Philadelphia Life Center has existed about eight years, and it is now possible to make some tentative generalizations about the relationships that have grown and changed with it. Without being final about what we say when we speak about "relationships in community," we hope that sharing some information and experience will be helpful to people who live in or are in the process of starting other social change communities.

KINDS OF RELATIONSHIPS

In the Life Center, people connect with each other in different ways and for different purposes. Each implies a different kind of relationship. The first part of this paper describes some of the relationships that happen most frequently. There may be several kinds that happen between any two people.

Housemates: Members of a communal household by necessity have some kind of relationship with each other. That varies according to the nature of the community and people's inclinations. All houses require cooperation for common functions such as cooking, cleaning, maintenance and repair, and sharing common space. In addition, most houses in the Life Center provide regular sharing times in house meetings and retreats and ongoing support for their members.

These basic necessities dictate certain requirements of household relationships. People need to be compatible with each other. That means being able to work easily together on common house tasks, feeling comfortable around each other and able to communicate and take an interest in each other's lives, and having similar ideas about common concerns such as food, house expenditures, standard of living, and interior decoration.

There are close relationships that happen within a communal household. Some of these existed prior to moving into the community; others may develop. There have been restrictions in some Life Center households against sexual relationships starting between housemates, on the grounds that it causes divisiveness and jealousies. Other houses have been more relaxed, and relationships have not caused major difficulties. Members of a community in formation need to decide what their tolerance is for dealing with potentially confusing relationships in their own house. Close relationships in a house can be important and even help build a sense of community—as long as the two people do not become totally preoccupied with each other to the exclusion of their housemates. This can be a source of resentment. Resentment can often be avoided if people in a relationship communicate about it with their housemates and are responsible about the friendships they have with other people in the house.

If one person is involved in two serious relationships in her/his house, complications tend to multiply. This isn't to say it's impossible, but it requires understanding feelings and dealing with them responsibly. Other housemates need to be considered. The importance of any particular relationship needs to be balanced by a sense of responsibility to the whole community. It is difficult to live in a house where some of the members are in frequent emotional turmoil over each other. "Safety" is an important ingredient of a communal house. People need to be able to come home to a relaxed environment, where they feel cared about and supported. They do not want to be bombarded with problems or met with hostile silence.

It is *not* necessary or even advisable that everyone in a communal household be a close friend of everyone else. In addition to safety in their house people have a need for space, both psychic and physical. Particularly if a person leads a demanding life outside the house, she or he needs to have time at home when people are not making demands on her/his energy. Some people in the Life Center maintain their serious relationships outside of their own house. This guarantees that they will continue to lead lives of their own, and can get away from each other. It means that if they are having difficulties with each other, they still have a set of relaxed supportive relationships with their housemates to remind them that their lives are not a shambles.

People often try to keep their living and working relationships separate. It is rare that most people in a particular house also work together. In the Life Center political work is done in collectives, and collective members usually live in different houses from each other. If they do not, they try to make agreements about when they will and will not talk about work.

Work Relationships: Our purpose in community is to provide support for acting together to change our environment. In the political work done out of the Life Center we seek to develop work relationships that recognize human beings as ends in themselves not to be manipulated for political purposes. When we work together we focus not just on "the task," but on developing healthy work relationships.

We work together in an egalitarian way; making decisions by consensus, making sure everyone has a chance to participate. Some people need encouragement to participate more and have more confidence in themselves. People who have skills work at sharing them thoughtfully and patiently with people who don't. People who have been taught that they need to work hard and be leaders in order to be loved tend to work compulsively. They need to be encouraged and even pressured to slow down and to let others take responsibilities.

People schedule into business meetings time for personal sharing so that people will feel in touch with each other's lives. Time is given for feelings that come up over "hot" issues or conflicts with fellow workers. This does not mean that we "give in" to negative feelings and lose sight of what we're about. We *do* acknowledge that people respond emotionally, that we are all overcoming hurtful experiences in our past. Such feelings need to be dealt with, since they can easily get in the way. One collective takes a part of their regular weekly meeting time as "warm fuzzy time," during which one person shares important things that are happening in her/his life. Another collective does regular "estimation/self-estimations," in which members share things they think they are doing well and areas where improvement is needed. In each case the other collective members listen and then share their own thoughts about the person, her/his life, future directions, and efforts to grow.

Therapeutic relationships: Many people at the Life Center do Re-evaluation Counseling with each other on a regular basis. This is a form of peer counseling where people, usually in pairs, take turns being client and counselor. The purpose of the counseling is to feel and "discharge," through laughter, tears, anger, shivering, etc., painful feelings from the past that keep us from being completely alive and functioning in the present. This is a unique kind of relationship, very important in this community. Co-counselors try to keep their counseling relationship distinctly separate from other relationships they have with each other as workers or friends. People who get to know each other through counseling do not develop other kinds of relationships with each other. "Co-counselors" are committed to helping each other climb out of difficult feelings and unhealthy patterns of behavior.

Married couples: So far, few people have gotten married while living in the Life Center. People tend to be critical of marriage and the tradition of male domination that has accompanied it. Needs for love and companionship in general do not all get placed on one other person. Most people have a valuable network of friendships and associations. Some of these may be more important or have a greater sense of permanence than others, but they rarely approximate the model of a traditional marriage.

Married or unmarried, couples who move into a Life Center house have usually been living in situations where they depended almost exclusively on each other for meeting personal needs. In community that is no longer necessary. They are surrounded by people ready to be their friends, to offer nurture and friendly challenges. Each person in a couple may discover needs and interests that can be pursued independently of the other. Each person may develop a slightly different circle of friends and begin spending increasing amounts of social and work time with them.

This tendency can have positive effects on the people in a couple relationship. They usually begin to realize that, while they love each other, much of the time they have spent with each other has been at the expense of pursuing personal strength and independence from each other. Their demands for time and attention from each other beome fewer and less stringent.

Quite likely each will begin to seek questioning and feedback about the relationship, leading to serious reflecting and evaluating. This evaluating will gradually begin to work changes. The woman may begin to develop friendships with other women and become involved in feminist activities. The man may join a men's group. Sexist dynamics in the relationship will certainly be pointed out.

This is a creative process! Understandably, however, it *can* be upsetting and even threatening. One or both may begin to wonder what has happened to the relationship and why they don't spend as much time together as they used to. What *is* happening? Usually two things. First, changes are happening in each person that have implications for the relationship. Secondly, there is less time spent and less attention given to each other than previously. As a result, they can get badly out of touch. Furthermore, both are probably discovering that, while there is respect in the community for their relationship, they are regarded and affirmed primarily as individuals, *not* as members of a couple. Being part of a larger collective group like a communal house requires a strong individual identity in relation to that group. People in that group want to hear their individual thoughts in decision-making, and to agree or disagree with them individually. Couples acting as a "bloc" within the group can create an unhealthy power dynamic that will stir resentment among other house members.

It is healthy that couples who enter community pursue their individuality. One danger is that they may begin avoiding each other. The new friendships they both form may seem fresher, less restrictive, more rewarding, and more reflective of the changes that are happening to them. The old relationship may seem deadening and unresponsive by comparison. Both may be very conscious of the problems and old patterns of behavior, the heavy expectations that accompany the relationship. It's much easier to opt for the new friendships.

No doubt it's true that changes should be made in the old relationship. At some point the relationship may even need to end, or at least take a new form. On the other hand there can be strong reasons for maintaining it and working it out. Chances are that both people know each other very well. Once they free themselves of old resentments or unreasonable expectations of each other, they can be enormously helpful in pushing each other to grow in areas that have been difficult in the past. They may understand things about each other that are perplexing and take a long time for other people to grasp. Undoubtedly they both love each other a lot, and underneath old feelings of hurt there is a willingness to nurture and support each other.

For couples to be helpful to each other in these ways, encouragement from others is needed. The woman needs to know that she will not have the same crushing burden of meeting her husband's emotional needs that she had before moving into community. The man needs to know that he will not be expected to play the role of provider and protector. The relationship can continue with the clear understanding that they are separate individuals with individual lives, and that their priorities are their own personal growth and fulfillment.

Other Intense Relationships: Some relationships between people in the Life Center are more serious and long-term than others. Some start out being long-term and end rather quickly. Some begin slowly and unpretentiously, perhaps growing out of a work relationship or some other connection, and gradually take on the appearance of a solid, durable friendship.

There seems to be considerable variety in relationships at the Life Center. There tends also to be flexibility within any particular one, so that it may change a lot over a period of time. It may be sexual for a while, then the couple may decide to change it into a less intense friendship.

While people generally seek alternatives to traditional marriage, we learned long ago that the alternative to "lifetime commitment" is not complete absence of commitment. In the beginning of a relationship and at various points in its progress couples try to clarify what their mutual expectations are. This is often done with the help of a third neutral party. Sometimes formal contracts are established which state clearly what can and cannot be expected in the relationship, and a time is set for review and evaluation. Agreements may be changed after stated periods, according to changing needs. It is not always done this formally; written contracts are made when it seems likely that each person will have very different expectations.

"Multiple Relationships": It is not uncommon in this community for one person to be involved at one time in more than one close, loving relationship. The relationships may or may not be sexual and may change from time to time. Since people need physical closeness, these relationships may include physical appreciation of each other and sleeping together. While "multiple" relationships" used to be regarded as almost inherently traumatic in the Life Center, that is less so now. Part of the difficulty has been dealing with the expectations we were raised with which said that good people don't love

more than one person at a time. There are more and more healthy examples of people involved in more than one loving, growing relationship. This makes it easier for other people to relax and allow *their* love to flow more freely.

However, people must assess responsibly what they are ready to take on in relationships. It is not particularly empowering to get involved in more relationships than you have psychic or emotional energy for. If relationships are not enjoyable and strengthening, they defeat their purpose.

Sexual jealousies tend to be strong in multiple relationships. If all the relationships operate in the same house, this can be especially difficult. People involved must communicate openly about what does and does not feel good. It is also good to avoid the tendency to "heaviness"—treating the relationships as if they were the most serious things in the world.

Women Loving Women, Men Loving Men: Because the Life Center as a community has a strong commitment to working on sexism, heterosexual couples work hard at breaking out of traditional sex roles. The growth of feminism and the women's movement in the Life Center has increased that commitment tremendously. It has also increased the tendency of women to develop loving relationships with each other. Women increasingly have come to see themselves as self-sufficient and independent from men, able to nurture, love and support each other. This provides them strength for building a liberating women's movement dedicated to breaking down sex roles and patriarchy and creating a new identity for women.

Increasingly men are building friendships and supportive relationships with each other. Men's consciousness-raising groups and the growth of the men's movement has begun to make clear to men that they are capable of trusting and loving each other. They do not need to turn automatically to women for their nurturing. Women increasingly have begun demanding that men look to each other's needs and support each other, since women need their energy for their own liberation. Gradually and with much difficulty, men are learning to relax and trust each other and acknowledge love for each other in ways that are sensitive and appreciative.

Adults and Children: More and more thinking and effort is being given to improving relationships between adults and children. Parents in the community have in the past often felt saddled by the lack of support and assistance in child-rearing. More and more in houses where there are children, there is thought being given to the tendency of adults to regard children as nuisances or as less than human. House meetings are scheduled to talk about difficulties in relating to the children, and awareness is increasing that children are an oppressed group of people who require special thinking and awareness on the part of adults.

There was at one time in the community a system of "godparents," whereby an adult agreed to spend some amount of time each week with one particular child, developing a long-term friendship with her/him. This system worked with varying degrees of success. When the adult allowed the time with the child to operate on the child's terms as well as her/his own, things went well. Since people tend to be busy at the Life Center, and since children tend to get put low on people's priorities, unless they are parents the time was usually rushed and less than satisfactory.

COMPONENTS OF GOOD RELATIONSHIPS

While there are many kinds of relationships that operate within the Life Center, there are some basic components that seem important to relationships in general, with variation depending on what kind of relationship it is.

1) Each person in a relationship needs to recognize the basic freedom and individuality of both members. This means no agreements get made that subordinate important parts of one person's growth in the interests of the other's needs. Each person is her/his own first concern and responsibility.

2) Each person takes responsibility for her/his own feelings. People must recognize that their feelings in relation to another person may or may not be an accurate reading of the real situation. Feelings should be thought about carefully before they are acted on.

3) "Needs" must be defined clearly and agreed upon as appropriate before a person can expect the other to respond to them. In a specific situation a person should state what they need and not expect or demand that this other person intuit it. At times a person will be unable to do this and the other person will have to guess or

"feel" what is right, but that should not become the norm.

What needs are appropriate? It is possible to name at least some of them. People need companionship and closeness to other people. They need aware and loving physical contact. They need a chance to share their thinking and learn from other people's ideas. They need love and affirmation. They need their friends to see them clearly and love them despite their problems or obnoxious patterns of behavior. They need to believe that they are not going to be abandoned and left alone because they are not acceptable as people. They need to be encouraged and even pushed to grow, often in ways that are initially painful. They need to have fun, to be able to enjoy themselves in the company of other people.

4) Equality is the basic principle in good relationships. Specifically that means that a relationship does not exist primarily for the benefit of one person, but is mutually supportive and challenging. Each person thinks about the other and shares the responsibility for sustaining all parts of the relationship.

5) Each person in a relationship must keep in touch with the unique identity of the other person, and not get them confused with someone else in their life, past or present.

BARRIERS TO GOOD RELATIONSHIPS

What gets in the way of all these things happening naturally and easily? We assume that these are components that we all want in our relationships. When we think about what makes this difficult, several kinds of hurts or oppressions, imposed on us at various points in our lives by our environment, can be identified as causes.

Sexism: This is a primary one. Women in our society have been defined primarily as servants, supporters, and nurturers of men. This denies them the chance to discover who they are and what their lives might be like, and to pursue their own interests independently of the interests of men.

Men are taught to be aggressive, competitive, "self-reliant," and in control. The result is that they alienate themselves from everyone else in society, including other men, by playing a dominant and oppressing role. They rely blindly on women to meet their emotional needs, since they have not learned to do that for themselves, or for each other.

Unless a community focuses attention on sexism consciously and makes a common decision to work hard against it, most men will automatically gravitate to women for attention, listening, and suppport. A woman may look for a relationship with a man in order to feel secure, cared about, and protected. It makes sense for people in the community or household to question people in this kind of relationship. Dynamics operating that are clearly sexist should be interrupted.

In the Life Center women's support groups, a feminist collective and the gay caucus create safe environments in which women share thinking and strategy in combatting sexism and building closer relationships with each other. Men are assuming more responsibility for interrupting sexism operating in their brothers and for helping other men deal with their feelings. This is important as women they relate to begin to withdraw traditional feminine types of support and get closer to other women.

Ageism: Discriminating or putting people in rigid roles or categories on the basis of their age is another barrier to healthy relationships. Most adults have difficulty relating to children as full, equal human beings. The reason for that is that none of us were treated as responsible people when we were children. So we repeat toward children the same hurtful behavior that was directed at us when we were young.

Ageism directed towards older people tends to stereotype them as "retired," as having outlived their usefulness and productivity. This society places a high premium on being young. Things are changing fast, so the information and experience that older people have does not always seem particularly relevant. Often this is a false assumption.

In the Life Center relationships between young and older adults approximate peer relationships more closely than in most places in the society. There is a danger of slipping into parent-child or even grandparent-grandchild roles, but we are learning that people of very different ages and experience can perceive and relate to each other as equal human beings. It is also helpful for older people to find support among themselves. There is here a group of older women who meet regularly, calling themselves "WOW": Wonderful Older Women!

"Old Needs and Hurts": There are many kinds of "old hurts" that we have experienced that rear their heads in various unpleasant ways when we try to relate to people in the present. All of us had needs at various times in our growing up that did not get met. These tend to attach themselves to our personalities and become fixtures. If we're not aware of them and how they operate they can create difficulties.

One way this happens is in trying to find one person who will meet all of our needs, who will finally love us just exactly the way we really want to be loved. This syndrome can cause a person to move from one relationship to the next, continually frustrated because no one seems to do it quite right. No one loves us the way we wanted our father or mother or older brother to.

Another way old needs can crop up is in feelings of jealousy and competition. These feelings come out of a fear that love is a scarcity—"there just isn't enough of it to go around and if I don't grab a hold of someone really tight and hold on, there isn't going to be enough for me." Operating under this set of assumptions, a person feels threatened when a loved one loves and is loved by another person. It is difficult not to fear being left or abandoned, that secretly "she loves him more than she does me." If the feelings are strong enough and have no outlet they can cause torment for the person and drive friends to exasperation. Nearly everyone is susceptible to feelings of jealousy or competition, especially when someone they love is in a relationship with someone else.

Another way that old hurts can appear in present relationships is in the continual demand to "prove that you love me." Someone may ask for reassurance in many different ways, but none is ever quite convincing enough. The person may conclude that they really are not loved after all if certain things are not done—if a certain ritual is not performed, if they are challenged on something, or told "no, I don't want to spend time with you now."

WHAT IS DONE WITH FEELINGS?

We assume that people who act in ways that are sexist or ageist, who dominate or allow themselves to be dominated, who feel competitive or consistently unloved, do so because they are trapped by their feelings. They have been hurt repeatedly in the past in ways that restrict their ability to love and be loved. This becomes especially obvious in a community such as this one. People are not expected to love just one person in one particular kind of way. Our loving works through lots of different kinds of relationships with different people. People are stretched by that experience, and expected to work on the things that restrict them.

There is a dangerous tendency in relationships to act on feelings without being aware that they are there. Some people may structure their whole lives around doing things that will *make* other people love them, without fully realizing that they're trapped by the feeling that people *don't* love them. People in the Life Center try to be aware of what their feelings are, and how those feelings act as a force in their relationships. It is helpful to share that information with the other person in a relationship, so that they can understand when a friend acts or feels in a way that seems inappropriate. Recognizing feelings and acknowledging them is an important first step.

There is an understanding in the community that feelings should be examined carefully before they are acted upon. Where is my anger coming from in this discussion? Is it really directed at her/him or is it coming up from previous talks that this reminds me of, that were frustrating and difficult for me? People try to avoid "dumping," or unloading all of their feelings at a particular moment on another person. It is often difficult to separate our thinking and our true perceptions of the present situation from old hurtful feelings that pull at us and demand that we act in certain ways.

Re-evaluation counseling is a way many people in the community deal with feelings. In counseling sessions people are encouraged to go back to the old memories that still carry pain with them, and they cry and rage and tremble and laugh until the pain relaxes and they are freed from the grip of the old memories. This is often a very long process. Fortunately, people don't have to be completely free from old hurts to have good relationships in the present. Once people have identified where their feelings come from and are working on them in counseling sessions, they can feel themselves "winning" and assume that they won't be trapped by them forever. This frees them to act in ways that are flexible and appropriate to the present.

It is in large part this kind of clarity about feelings and what to do with them that allows relationships in the Life Center to flourish. If feelings are not dealt with well, communities can dissolve or simply flounder and come to a stop, as immense amounts of energy are consumed dealing with the challenging new relationships people form.

People forming new communities must realize that they will not be able to satisfy everyone's apparent emotional "needs," stated or unstated. All it takes is one person who demands that every feeling they have to be assuaged or responded to by community members to send everyone flying in different directions. It is important for people to be clear when they are living in community about what their limits are in dealing with the relationships they have with people in it.

A FINAL WORD

These thoughts are shared on the basis of one set of experiences in one community. The information may be helpful to people forming other communities. We'd like to say to you, "Don't be intimidated!" Don't feel you need to duplicate someone else's experience. Your community will grow if you tend it responsibly, watching out for pitfalls, and keeping your vision in mind. We hope this paper will help you do that.

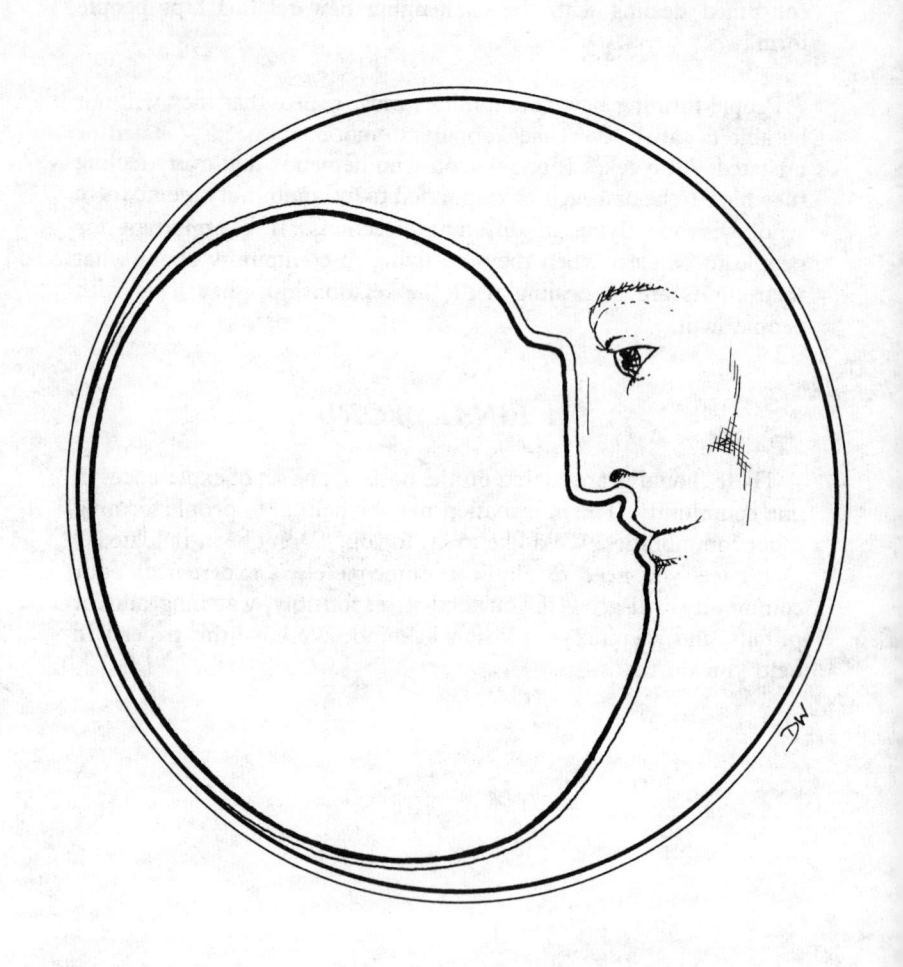

CHAPTER 7
CREATIVE CONFLICT RESOLUTION

We all encounter conflicts in our daily lives—conflicts between children, between children and adults, between spouses, between adults living together in the same household, or between fellow workers or group members. The problem for all of us is learning how to handle conflict creatively so that we, and the people we are in conflict with, can grow and resolve our differences and not be stifled in our development by poor methods of responding or rigid solutions which do not meet our needs. As people working for change we will not only need to learn how to respond to conflict, but how to bring it into the open, encourage it, and then use it as an integral part of the change process.

This chapter is an effort to share some of the experience of the Training/Action Affinity Group in working with conflict—both within the Philadelphia Life Center and with social change groups elsewhere. At the Life Center, the Affinity Group has had extensive experience helping communal households deal with internal conflicts. We have also worked with various collectives to resolve specific conflicts and to set up regular processes that surface conflicts early. In addition, the Affinity Group has worked with numerous groups throughout the United States who have been trying to work towards important societal change. Our role there has been to help them develop skills in clarifying their own goals, nurturing the individuals in the group, and resolving conflicts as they arise. This chapter includes both a theoretical discussion of the dynamics of conflict and some specific, practical ways to work on conflicts. This chapter is in six parts:

I. An Approach to Conflict Resolution
II. Dimensions of Conflict
III. Conflict Analysis
IV. The Stages and Dynamics of Conflict Resolution

V. The Role of a Third Party Neutral in Conflict Resolution
VI. Processes for Resolving Conflicts Between Individuals or with Groups or Households

AN APPROACH

Why is conflict resolution important in an intentional community, a collective or network of people working for social change? When a group of adults and children decide to live together, work together in a collective, or share a common commitment to social change, there are bound to be some disagreements and hot conflicts. Each member has different values, experiences, needs and ideas about how things should be done. Conflict resolution skills are important for several reasons. First, on the personal level, it is more enjoyable to live in a house where individual relationships are not constantly rocked by conflict. Skill in handling conflicts allows individuals and the group to be pushed to change while still providing a safe and stable environment in which to live. In a social change community, conflicts within a household or collective can come to absorb vast amounts of time and energy that would otherwise be directed towards the political work at hand. If we develop our skills at handling such internal questions we will have more energy to be effective change agents.

On the political level, conflict resolution is important because it:
1) Demonstrates to others that conflicts can be resolved creatively and nonviolently.
2) It shows that we can all learn and develop skills for handling conflicts.
3) It allows an individual to handle conflicts creatively in her/his personal life while continuing to work for basic social change.
4) It provides us with the confidence we need to actively engage in conflicts with the world around us since conflict is a basic ingredient in any work for social change.

What is Conflict?

"Social conflict is a relationship between two or more (people) who *believe* they have incompatible goals." It is a form of competition. Conflict occurs in what Adam Curle calls an "unpeaceful relationship." An unpeaceful relationship "exists whenever an individual's potential development, mental or physical, is held back by the conditions of the relationship."[2]

For example, a nuclear family which had had no previous communal experience decided to move into a communal household. The husband expected to maintain traditional sex roles in that he expected his wife to cook, clean, and emotionally care for him. The woman and the other members of the house had different ideas; they expected everyone to share equally in house maintenance tasks and to share emotional support for each other too. The man in this situation clearly was in a conflict with other members of his house. All the people involved believed that they had incompatible goals. The conflict also illustrates an unpeaceful relationship in which the woman was held back from her potential development by her husband's belief and practice of societal sex roles. There was a conflict of goals in that the woman needed the time which she would have to spend for her husband's upkeep for her own development, and she needed him to be responsible for himself. He, on the other hand, did not want to take the time to be involved in doing house maintenance chores (and also, in this case, he did not feel skilled in cooking). Because he was unwilling to cooperate he was being held back in his relationships with other house members as well as maintaining oppressive sex roles.

Some Assumptions About Conflict

People's attitudes toward conflict affect how they act or behave in a conflict situation, how they handle their feelings, the process they set up to resolve conflicts, and ultimately the solutions that they can select.

There are several assumptions about conflict which our experience in community seems to confirm. These assumptions have greatly facilitated our handling of conflict.

1) *Conflict is a natural occurence* and will always be with us. Our task is to learn to respond to conflicts in the most creative ways possible. Conflict is an integral part of the change process.

2) *Conflict is one way that individuals and communities grow.* Conflict is a process in which different viewpoints or actions struggle with each other, are merged, and form new ideas of human behavior.

3) *Conflicts arise because people believe that they have incompatible goals.* Conflicting goals may demand either changed behavior or changed values.

4) *Social structure,* or the ways that relationships in a community or collective are put together (or not put together), frequently cause conflicts.

5) *Conflicts should not be glossed over* or allowed to build up. They should be worked on as they arise. Open conflict appears because individuals or groups realize they are being oppressed and move to change the situation. The goal of conflict resolution is for the individuals involved to move toward a relationship where each can develop to her/his greatest potential.

6) *Conflicts have predictable dynamics and cycles.* They can be regulated to minimize damage to individuals and groups and to maximize growth and benefits for all concerned.

7) *Feelings are an integral component of conflicts.* Feelings and rational thinking are not the same. One should not act on feelings without considering where the feelings come from and whether the feelings coincide with a well-thought-out plan of action. Feelings cannot be solved; issues and behavior problems can be.

DIMENSIONS OF CONFLICT

There are five major factors which influence the dimensions of conflicts: awareness of conflict, intensity of feelings and actions, rules or customs which regulate how conflicts are resolved, the purity of conflict, and the levels of power inequality.[3]

Awareness—Awareness refers to the recognition by one or both of the people or groups involved that a conflict, or incompatible goals, exist. Frequently it takes one person or group to identify that a conflict exists and then to force the conflict into the open so that the other party can see the disagreement. Incompatible goals can be present and an unpeaceful relationship exist without one or both of the people involved recognizing the fact. It takes one of the people involved to identify the conflict and to call it to the attention of the other community member before a conflict can move from a submerged state to an open state.

Occasionally a situation arises in which one or both of the people involved *think* that they are in conflict with each other when the objective facts indicate that there is not a conflict. This type of conflict awareness, false conflict awareness, may cause people to act as if they have incompatible goals. Some of the causes for false conflict awareness include: misinformation, an inaccurate understanding of the social situation, or feelings about similar circumstances in the past. In this latter case the feelings are connected with the past event and may or may not be directly linked to the present experience. The feelings create a situation in which it *feels* as if a real conflict exists when in fact the proper conditions are not present.

Intensity—The intensity of a conflict refers to level of feelings (strong and mild) and of behavior (actively violent to passive) that are present in a conflict. Although feelings do not have to affect the behavior present in a conflict, they frequently do. Generally, the greater the intensity of feelings, the greater the possibility of violent or aggressive behavior.

It must be noted that "in relationships where the participants are engaged with their total personality rather than with only a segment of it, there will probably arise feelings of love and hatred, both attraction and hostility."[4] Living in community, like any close relationship, is likely to generate more intense feelings than casual friendship relations. Because there is greater investment in relationships where the total personality is involved, the risk of conflicts which would disturb the relationships are greater. Greater risk may lead to build and to intensify with time. Intensity can be lowered by dealing with conflicts as they arise rather than accumulating feelings.

Regulation of Conflict—Sometimes rules or customs that either were agreed upon by individuals or are values of the community influence the way conflicts are resolved. The rules may define what kinds of power are acceptable in relationships, what kind of force is used to reach a goal, and when force can be used. For example, in several of the Life Center households there is a growing awareness of children's liberation. One aspect of this liberation is that children should be involved in defining the rules by which they live. Thus the parents of a pre-teenage child have worked out with their daughter a set of rules for when she should be home at night, where she is allowed to visit in the evenings, and when she should call to let them know where she is. The rules also include agreed-upon punishments if the rules are violated.

Conflict regulation agreements may be informal internalized values or formal written statements.

Power Inequality—Power refers to the strength that one person or group has to force or convince another person or group to do something. Power can be defined only in relation to another person's power.

Factors that influence one person's power over another's include:
1) the psychological or physical cost which both people involved are willing to incur to get their way.
2) The amount that both people are willing to suffer to get their way.
3) How important the issue at stake is to both people.

Assessing who has more power is frequently difficult; testing or direct confrontation is often necessary for the people or parties involved to judge each other's relative power and to determine how important the issue in contention is to each of them. For example, when Peter's father tells him that he cannot watch TV now and that he must come down for dinner, and Peter refuses and says, "I won't come... no matter what you do!" Peter is testing his father's power. Adults do the same thing in their relationships with each other. "Degrees of power differences can affect awareness of the conflict by both parties, how the parties reach agreement to terminate the conflict, what the outcome is likely to be, and even whether an underlying conflict exists."[5]

Conflict Analysis

In approaching a particular conflict it is often helpful to break the problem into component parts so that we can see what is happening at any stage of its development and/or resolution. The Conflict Chart (See pages 64-65) is a useful tool which can be used in combination with the Conflict Questions to analyze conflict development and dynamics. The following description of the components of a conflict is in greater detail than the information on the chart.

History—Every conflict has a history of events or relationships which have led up to the present crisis. It is important to understand what has happened in the past in order to understand the present situation.

People involved—Another factor to identify is who is involved in the conflict. Who are the central actors, peripheral people, interested people, potential allies, or third parties? In any conflict it is critical to identify "Who owns the problem," in order to decide who should be involved in the solution.[6]

Social Environment—Every conflict occurs in the context of some form of social relationship. There may be rules or regulations which limit a conflict. Can these rules be recognized or identified? Is the conflict sporadic, in that it occurs infrequently, or is it the kind of conflict that is always present?

Issues, Goals, and Needs—On every conflict there are issues, or problems around which the conflict is focused, present. Community members all also have specific goals or outcomes which they would like to have happen. Goals can be based upon wishes of the people in the conflict or upon concrete needs that they feel. A solution to a conflict depends upon the correct identification of issues, goals, and needs by the people involved in the conflict or a third party who has agreed to help.

Issues may include value conflicts, such as survival values where one community member wants to have the right to stay in the community, conflicts over ideology, welfare values which include needs for material goods or personal growth, or authority issues such as the right to make one's own decisions.

In analyzing a conflict it is important to distinguish between realistic issues which are of genuine concern to the people in the conflict, and non-realistic issues which have low content value but are used as an excuse to vent anger in front of the opponent.[7]

Another aspect of issues is the tendency for a conflict based on a specific complaint ("You didn't take out the garbage!") to expand ("And you didn't wash the floor or do child care, or wash the dishes..."). The tendency of an issue to move from a specific complaint to a general complaint about a multitude of sins that the other person has committed is commonly called "gunny-sacking."[8] It is important to separate issues and handle them at one time.

Feelings—Whenever there is a conflict there are feelings present. People experience feelings because of irritation, fear, anger, hurt, frustration, etc., around the present conflict or because there are old feelings left over from similar conflict situations in the past. The latter form of feelings is called restimulation.

CONFLICT DEVELOPMENT

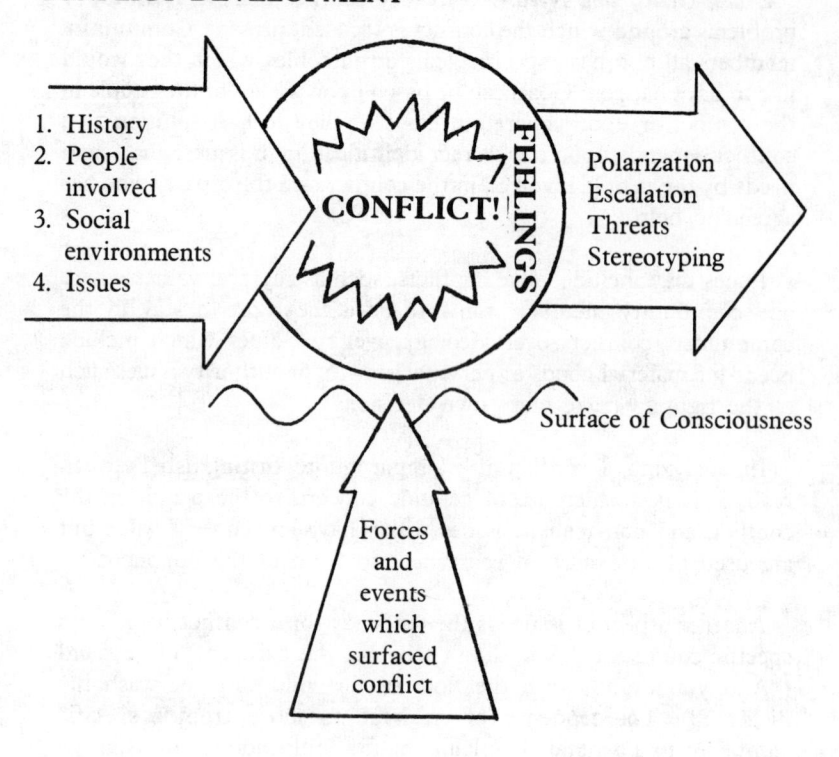

→ 1. History
2. People involved
3. Social environments
4. Issues

CONFLICT! *FEELINGS*

→ Polarization
Escalation
Threats
Stereotyping

Surface of Consciousness

↑ Forces and events which surfaced conflict

CONFLICT ANALYSIS QUESTIONS:

1. What is happening? — feelings, history, events, behavior
2. Who are the people involved?
3. What surfaced the conflict so that both people involved recognized it?
4. What are the issues, goals, and needs of the people in the conflict?
5. How can the problem be broken into solvable parts?

I. CONCILIATION
1. Making contact
2. Handling feelings
3. Building trust
4. Agreements to Talk
5. Guidelines for negotiation

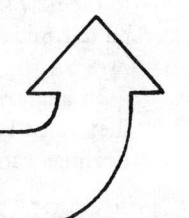

PROCESSES OF RESOLUTION

II. NEGOTIATION
1. Clarify what happened
2. Clarify issues, goals, and needs
3. Divide problem into smaller parts
4. Select one of the parts, or subproblems, and generate solutions
5. Select a solution
6. Restate agreement

III. IMPLEMENTATION
1. I.D. steps for implementation
2. Review what each person has agreed to do
3. I.D. where help is needed
4. Set evaluation date and time
5. Evaluate whole conflict resolution process

It is important to recognize that feeling feelings is different from thinking, which is intellectual activity. Decisions or actions which are based purely on feelings may not be "rational" decisions. Frequently strong feelings block creative thinking and problem solving in conflict situations by locking people into rigid behavior (behavior shaped by past bad experiences) rather than allowing them to respond to the new situation as a completely new experience. Feelings should be felt but not necessarily acted upon.

In analyzing a conflict it is important to identify feelings because they must be responded to and vented *before* issues can be resolved. Feelings cannot be resolved; they can only be felt.

Conflict Dynamics—Conflicts frequently follow a sequence of events, early events which build tension, an event or events which pushes the conflict into the open so that both parties recognize it, an escalation of tension with a corresponding increase of intense feelings and a greater possibility of violent actions, a venting of feelings, events which limit the scope of the conflict, and a de-escalation of tension. It is important to identify what events have occurred in a conflict so that you know how to respond.

In any type of conflict several events or one major event usually bring a conflict into the open so that both people or groups involved recognize that a conflict exists. People who are interested in aggressive non-violent conflict resolution will note the similarity to direct action where one group creates a crisis which forces the opponent to recognize an injustice. In personal relationships it may be necessary to precipitate a crisis event, or it may occur spontaneously, in order to raise consciousness about an issue.

Normally conflicts are either hidden under the surface of our consciousness and appear in the form of mild irritation, hurt or anger; or they are consciously recognized by one or both of the people or groups involved but are suppressed for fear that they will damage the relationship or destroy the peace. Conflict resolution requires open recognition of conflicts.

After the initial crisis there may be a period of escalation in which the parties may escalate threats, see each other in stereotyped ways or even adopt each others' mannerisms or tactics. "Well if you are going to play dirty, I can play dirty too!" The people involved may gunnysack, see the problem as a complete polarization of viewpoints, and may attack the other person's integrity rather than the issue itself.

After escalation, what can be done? This is the subject of the remaining part of this chapter.

THE STAGES AND DYNAMICS OF CONFLICT RESOLUTION

There are not techniques that guarantee solutions that will be satisfactory to all of the people involved in a conflict, but there are some guidelines and processes which certainly facilitate resolution. Conflict resolution may be divided into three major steps: conciliation, negotiation/bargaining, implementation of the solution, and evaluation.

Conciliation—Conciliation could be defined as action which psychologically prepares people to change their relationship to one another.[9] Conciliation can occur with or without the presence of a neutral third person who is not involved in the conflict.

There are five important aspects of conciliation:
1) *Making contact* between the people who are in conflict.
2) *Handling the feelings* of the conflicting people.
3) *Building trust*—dissolving stereotypes, affirming the good aspects of the people in the conflict, identifying points which the people hold in common, and affirming the relationship itself.
4) *Getting the conflicting parties to agree* to talk about the feelings and the issues.
5) *Setting up guidelines* for the discussion/negotiation.

All of the actions listed above are important steps in de-escalating a conflict on the feeling level. Once feelings are dealt with, the community members can move ahead to the negotiations which will restructure their relationship and eliminate the cause of the conflict.

1) *Making contact* between two people or groups of people who are in a conflict is one of the most difficult tasks. If the people involved are still talking to each other the problem is greatly facilitated, but if

the people or groups are refusing to communicate the task becomes more complicated. In either case, the problem is how to help the people involved handle their feelings so that they can begin to communicate and change the conditions which created the conflict. The initial breakthrough in communications may occur when one person involved says, "Listen, we really have to talk about this," and then makes the necessary arrangements for the conversation; or when a third party who is not involved in the conflict takes the initiative to intervene, talk to all the people involved, and set up the necessary conditions for conciliation and negotiation. The third party may or may not be invited to intervene by the people in the conflict. We will discuss the role of third party intervention in greater detail later under the "Role of a Third Party in Conflict Resolution."

2) *Feelings* cannot be resolved through negotiations; feelings can only be felt and vented. Conciliation is a time when all the members involved should be encouraged to vent, or release, their feelings about the conflict and about the people with whom they disagree in a safe and separate setting. The venting of the feelings has several functions. First, it allows people to "blow off steam" prior to meeting with each other to negotiate. Venting before meeting face-to-face helps to prevent community members from dumping intense feelings into the negotiation session, which may create more tension and make the conflict harder to resolve. Second, releasing feelings often relieves the tension that prevents people from thinking clearly about a conflict. Venting feelings often leads to new insights about the problem. Third, venting feelings often helps people stick to agreements that are made in the negotiating sessions. Frequently people involved in a conflict will reach an agreement or solution, but it will be difficult to get one or both parties to stick to it. Often agreements fail because people have not worked through feelings about the conflict and thus subconsciously block implementation.

How are feelings vented? In our community experience we have found a variety of ways to release feelings. Sometimes community members who are involved in a conflict go to separate rooms, either alone or with a neutral friend, and will blow off steam. They will shout, jump up and down, pound pillow, cry, etc., in an effort to release tension. Sometimes they find a friend and talk over the problem, taking special notice of the feelings that they feel.

One way that we have found helpful to work through feelings is a peer counseling discipline called Re-evaluation Counseling. It can be used to get rid of tension, hurt, anger, or fear around a conflict situation in the present. It is particularly helpful in identifying the past hurtful experiences that make it difficult to deal with the present conflict most creatively.[10]

For people who are not familiar with Re-evaluation Counseling or any similar discipline, it may be helpful to sit down with a friend and describe how it feels. The role of the friend is to listen and help clarify, not argue or persuade the person to feel otherwise. One useful technique is "active listening," a part of the Parent Effectiveness Training process that can be transferred to use with adults.[11]

3. *Building Trust*—The members of "the gathering," one of the communal households in the Philadelphia Life Center, were having lots of personal conflicts that were making life difficult for all of the people involved. Everyone was reluctant to talk about them because of fear or lack of trust that the issues would be dealt with sensitively. Finally one of the members suggested that each person take some time to acknowledge aloud their own fine qualities and the good parts of the relationships they had with other house members. After each person had spoken other house members were free to say good things about her/him about things that they had observed or felt. When all of the people had had a turn at this kind of "affirmation," the focus turned to the house as a whole. Everyone brainstormed a list of all the good things that were happening in the house. Having identified and publicly affirmed good things about each house member and the household as a whole, "the gathering" people began to raise the issues that they needed to talk about.

The exercise which "the gathering" members did illustrates several important components of trust building which is part of conciliation.

First, the exercise which allowed each house member to recognize good things about themselves and to have other house members affirm them created a positive atmosphere and raised the level of safety in the group. Second, the exercise identified things that each participant in the conflict had in common. It prevented the people from seeing others with whom they disagreed in a totally negative light. Third, the exercise gave each person a chance to share feelings and be heard as well as to listen to others.

Trust building occurs when individuals feel good about themselves, when people can identify points that they hold in common with individuals with whom they disagree, when people in a conflict can affirm their opponent, and when they can break down stereotypes of the opposition. The affirmation exercise used by the commune was one way to build trust. Informal talking can often serve the same function. In conflicts that involve intense feelings, a neutral third party may be helpful in developing trust between the people in conflict.

4. *Getting an agreement to talk* is the time when the people involved set up a concrete time to negotiate about the issues that are affecting their relationship. It is different from just making contact because it is the step that establishes the process by which the conflict will be resolved.

Sometimes it is very difficult to get people who are involved in a conflict to agree to talk about it. Failures at dialogue may be caused by:
1) Intense feelings by one or both of the people or groups which prevents them from talking productively about the problem.
2) Fear that the other people involved are not serious about negotiating.
3) Fear of the negotiation situation itself (either the environment is not safe or it is scary to speak in front of the conflicting person or group).
4) The lack of processes or procedures to handle the conflict.
5) The desire of one or more of the people or groups involved to *not* solve the problem (some people like to wallow in conflicts).

If one of the participants, or a third party, is having trouble establishing guidelines and an agreement to talk, consider the points listed above and/or ask the people involved what is blocking them from talking. Find solutions to the blocks before proceeding to the issues of the conflict.

5. Some guidelines for consideration when reaching an agreement to talk or negotiate are:
—*Set a specific time* and date.
—*Set a time limit* on the conversation so that one or both of the

people or groups involved are not worn down by the length of the discussions.
—*Set a time when both of the parties are not tired.* Late at night is generally not the best time to begin conflict resolution.
—*Set times for future discussions* of the problem or other problems which may arise during the present negotiations.
—*Define a process* or the steps that need to be taken in order to resolve the conflict—Who talks first? For how long? Rules about interruption, sarcasm, gunnysacking, etc.
—*Decide about a third party neutral*—Is one needed? Who would we like? Do they have the skill that we need?
—*Find a physical place that is safe* and neutral for both people or groups involved.
—*Establish a limit to discussion* so that the problem does not dominate all the other aspects of the people's lives.

Negotiation/Bargaining—A Process for Problem Solving— There are many books on negotiating and bargaining. If you are particularly interested in this step of conflict resolution, we recommend several good works in the bibliography at the end of the paper. In our experience, we have found five steps that are generally part of the negotiation process:

1) *Clarify what happened.* Each person or a representative of each group should be allowed time to describe how they see the conflict. History, precipitating events, crisis event(s), and feelings should be presented. The central issue and peripheral issues to the conflict should be identified and defined. In clarifying what happened, the people involved are building an argument for the goals and needs which they would like to see met.

2) Each person or group should *clarify what their goals and needs are.* Goals and needs may differ. It is important to realize that the goals and needs as stated at the beginning of the bargaining session are just that—an opening statement and not the final word. In the process of discussion the people involved may realize that certain goals or needs are not realistic and modify their expectations. One person may see that another's needs are greater than her/his and thus modify the position taken so that more needs can be met. (Note: Needs are not always rational. They may not be what the person needs to be happy or feel that a just settlement has been made. If in the context of the discussion irrational needs are uncovered, they

may be challenged; but challenging needs is a touchy job and requires a great deal of tact for a favorable outcome.)

3) *Divide the problem into several smaller problems.* See if there are component parts of the problem which can be identified and separated from the central issue. These smaller parts are frequently easier to solve than handling the whole problem at once. Also, handling some of the problem successfully, even though it is a small part, gives the people in the situation a feeling of success and encourages them to find solutions to other parts of the problem.

4) *Select one of the sub-problems and generate solutions for it.* Solutions may be generated by a process of "brainstorming" (an exercise in which people toss out ideas which are recorded but not commented upon until both people agree to discuss them); through conversation; through a process of individual reflection where each person involved in the conflict takes some time to think silently about solutions which would meet all the needs and then reports verbally back to the other person or group, etc.

5) *Select a solution.* Selection of a solution in the bargaining process is very much like making a consensus decision in a large group. An attempt should be made to synthesize and build on each person's ideas and information rather than choose one idea over another. The decision is one of persuasion rather than coercion.

In making a decision it is important to define long range goals for the relationship as well as short range goals. A decision should be consistent with both sets of goals for the relationship. If it is not, the end result will be more conflict in the future.

Upon solution of one problem return to step 4, select another and solve it.

Implementation—Frequently people involved in a conflict can agree to a solution but fail to implement it because they do not know how or fail to take the proper steps. In implementing a solution you should consider:
    a) What each group or person has agreed to do (the final agreement should be restated).
    b) How long they have agreed to do it for.
    c) What to do if a problem arises again.
    d) Whether either of the people or groups need any help in

order to adhere to or carry out the decision.
e) When to evaluate the solution to determine if any modifications or new solutions need to be found.

Evaluation—A formal evaluation is important because it provides an automatic opportunity for the people in the conflict to review the solution and make necessary modifications. Sometimes people are reluctant to settle a conflict because they are afraid that their decision will be final and not open to revision at a later time. An evaluation time when decisions can be reviewed eliminates this obstacle.

THE ROLE OF A THIRD PARTY NEUTRAL IN CONFLICT RESOLUTION

Conflicts which involve an individual and a group, or conflicts which involve two groups, are much more complex than disagreements between two individuals. The complexity is due to the greater number of feelings, goals, and needs of the community members.

In resolving these types of conflicts, as well as one-to-one conflicts with intense feelings involved, we frequently use a third party. Third parties are people who are not directly involved in the conflict who have agreed to play a variety of helping roles in resolving the dispute. Because we have found the use of the third party to be an effective aid in resolving conflicts, we would like to describe the roles and processes involved in this technique more fully.

Third parties can play conciliator roles, mediator roles, or both. Conciliator roles generally preceed the negotiations. Conciliation involves psychological preparation of the parties for dialogues with the people with whom they are in conflict. Mediation is the third party role which occurs during negotiations. Mediation involves a structured intervention between the people in the conflict, which helps them settle the dispute. Mediation and conciliation roles are frequently combined within the same person but this does not always have to be the case. For the purpose of this paper, we have divided the roles so that the tasks involved are more easily identified, and because we frequently ask different people to play different roles in actual practice.

Roles Outside of the Negotiation: Types of Conciliation and Tasks Involved

There are several roles which a third party can play outside of the negotiations. These roles include:

1) Conciliator—who helps one or both of the people or groups vent their feelings. This role can be performed by an interested listener, a Re-Evaluation Counselor, a person who has active listening skills. The task is to help the people in the conflict vent their feelings before negotiating so that they can think more clearly and not "dump" their feelings on the other people involved.
2) Conciliator—who helps clarify issues by reflecting the ideas of the people in the conflict back to them, by raising questions, by being a devil's advocate and reality tester, and by breaking stereotypes.

Both of these conciliator roles are generally played while the conflicting people are separated.

3) Conciliator—a go-between for the people who are in conflict who helps to set up negotiations.

Third Party Roles Inside the Negotiations

There are several kinds of third parties which may be involved when people are discussing or bargaining with each other. These include:

1) *Support Person*—person who generally does not speak during the bargaining session. His/her main function is to emotionally support one or both of the people or groups in conflict.
2) *Vibes Watcher*—person whose function is to watch for people's feelings, helps clarify feelings, and suggest processes which help people deal with emotions.
3) *Mediator/Facilitator*—person who has agreed to think about the process for resolving the conflict, facilitates the negotiation session, helps clarify feelings and issues, tries to identify points of agreement, suggests concrete steps for resolution of conflicts, restates settlement or agreement, helps define the steps for implementation of the agreements, facilitates evaluation.

It must be noted that the distinction between the vibes watcher and the mediator/facilitator is artificial and was done so that the roles could be clarified. In actual practice the two roles may be played by the same person or by a team of two people who alternate roles. The conciliator roles and the mediator/facilitator role may also be combined so that the person(s) who prepared the people for negotiations is also the one who mediates.

Examples: When Third Parties Have Been Used in Community

—Conflict about the amount of time a couple spend together:
   Conciliator helped them vent their feelings and to hear each other's needs more clearly.

—Conflict between one house member who needs quiet time and another house member who needs to use her stereo:
   Conciliator/Mediators helped both people and the rest of the house members vent their feelings and to negotiate an agreement.

—Conflict between all house members except one who is being asked to change or leave:
   Conciliators helped the individual and the house members to vent their feelings. Mediators facilitated the negotiations.

—One man challenging another man on issues of sexism:
   One person acted as vibes watcher and support person for both men involved.

—Many conflicts between all of the members of one household:
   Conciliator/Mediators provided personal support, attention so that people could vent their feelings and processes for examining and resolving conflicts.

—The dissolution of a communal household:
   Mediation/Facilitation team provided safety and processes for discussion of the dissolution, which was agreeable to all people involved.

Guidelines for Using a Third Party

1) Ask for help when you need it.

2) Define carefully the roles you need played.

3) If selecting a conciliator or mediator/facilitator both people or groups in the conflict must relate to, pick someone whom you both feel safe with and trust.

4) Select someone who can do the task you have defined.

5) Select someone that both people or groups feel is neutral to the particular conflict, and that both groups involved trust to remain neutral.

6) Contract an agreement with the third party regarding the role that you want her/him to play. All people must agree before the third party can act.

7) Allow the third party to play the role you have agreed upon.

8) If the people in the conflict or the third party feel that the third party role is not being performed correctly, the people involved are not cooperating with the third party, or more help is needed, the third party relationship should be ended or modified.

General Notes on Using and Being a Third Party

Frequently it is hard for people who are in conflict to ask for help from a third party. Some of the reasons for this problem include: "Wanting to handle the problem ourselves"; asking for help is frequently equated with failure; fear of being judged by a third party; fear that the third party will not be impartial; etc. These attitudes and feelings must be carefully examined and worked against when necessary. Third parties can be an effective aid in resolving conflicts, but people must be open to using third party help in order to benefit from their skills and presence.

Sometimes conflicts surface and there is not time to establish a formal third party role. In this type of situation, an interested bystander may take the initiative and become an impromptu conciliator or mediator. Uninvited third party intervention is risky and requires a great deal of sensitivity and insight into people and conflicts.

How do third parties get accepted by people in conflicts when the third party has been asked for help? In hot conflicts where there is potential for physical violence, a third party can sometimes gain credibility by the mere fact that she/he is there in the middle of the dispute. Presence may also draw hostility from the two people or groups in conflict toward the third party. This can have strategic advantages as well as disadvantages.

Another way to gain acceptance and credibility is to make a helpful observation or suggestion about how the conflict could be handled. If the suggestion is accepted, the credibility of the third party begins to grow. Each time the third party makes comment which is accepted by the people in the conflict, the authority of the third party increases. Informal third party relationships can become formal ones when the people or groups in a dispute ask the third party to play a definite role in the resolution process.

Frequently all the anger and frustration that the two people or groups involved in the conflict had been projecting on each other becomes directed at the impromptu third party. There are several possible causes for this response:
1) The conflicting people really don't want outside interference.
2) The third party was correct in his/her analysis or suggestion and has touched a raw nerve of the people in the conflict.
3) One of the people in the conflict feels that the third party is siding with the opposition.
4) It is easier and safer for the people in conflict to direct their anger on a third party (scapegoat) than toward each other.
5) The third party assessment of the situation was not accurate.

For whatever reason, impromptu third parties need to be prepared to have their services rejected. Rejection in some instances can be valuable because the third party can absorb some of the hostility and create the pre-conditions for the people in conflict to talk with each other.

PROCESSES FOR RESOLVING CONFLICTS BETWEEN INDIVIDUALS AND WITHIN GROUPS

The type of conflict resolution process used depends on the type of conflict—whether it is between two individuals, between one person and a group, or between two or more groups. There can also be multi-dimensional conflicts within groups. The processes which follow are ones we have used with individuals, groups and households both at the Philadelphia Life Center and elsewhere. Depending on the particular situation, steps are dropped or modified by the participants or by the third party neutral. We encourage you to do the same.

One-to-One Conflicts—This process of conflict resolution is useful for people who do not want to use a third party mediator. It is generally most successful when used on problems with a lower level of intense feelings, but may be used in "hot" situations too. It is a streamlined version of the previously mentioned steps to conflict resolution:

1) One person has gotten angry and has pushed the conflict into the open. The other person involved is angry too. Both agree to talk about it after venting their feelings.
2) People go to separate rooms and blow off steam. This may be done alone or with another person. The time allowed depends upon the intensity of the feelings.
3) One or both people present and agree to a process by which they will discuss the conflict—who goes first, rules for interruption, etc.
4) Each person takes an agreed-upon amount of time to describe without interruption how they see the conflict issues, goals, and their needs. *They do not speak for each other.* After each person has spoken, the other person repeats back what he or she has heard. This is to insure that both people are hearing each other. Both feelings and issues are listened to. They listen to feelings, but do not try to argue each other out of their feelings.
5) The parties talk about what both people need. They identify commmon needs and clarify any points of confusion.
6) The parties generate possible solutions to the conflict by brainstorming, reflecting and the sharing, or conversation.
7) They select one of the solutions either by a process of eliminating possibilities which neither can accept, by accepting a solution which they think they can both agree to, or by a combination of possible solutions. If they cannot accept any of the solutions they return to brainstorming more possibilities.
8) They figure out what has to be done to implement the

solution and set a date to evaluate how well the agreement has worked out.
9) The parties evaluate how this problem was handled and discuss how similar conflicts in the future can be responded to.
10) They do something out of the ordinary, like taking a walk or getting ice cream. They rest and celebrate the resolution.

Conflict Resolution Processes for Groups—The dynamics of group conflicts are similar to individual conflicts except that there are more feelings, goals, and issues present in group conflicts. There are also group behavior patterns, standardized responses of the group as a whole or between sub-groups, which also add to the complexity of a dispute. Examples of group patterns include: failure to deal with conflict as it arises; patterned speaking where one person speaks and the same person always comments; constant acceptance of put-downs.

Resolution of group conflicts follows the same general sequence of events as individual resolution. If a third party is not going to be used, a facilitator from within the group should carefully design the process for resolving the conflict before negotiating on issues. If a third party is used, the process may be looser and more flexible because a neutral is present who can think about the process as the discussions progress.

Following are several processes for surfacing and resolving conflicts.

A. **"Hypes 'n Gripes"** (to be used with or without facilitator)

    Purpose: To expose minor irritations or conflicts, to vent feelings, to have a complaint heard by the whole group.

    Set-up: In a group meeting ten minutes are set aside to do exercise. Five minutes are allowed for uninterrupted griping about things that are going badly in the house, frustrations, and minor conflicts. Gripes are given in brainstorm fashion *without comments* on each other's complaints. After five minutes everyone switches to "hypes," things that people like about each other and the house. (Be specific.) At the end of five minutes, check and see if any of the gripes need to be put on the meeting agenda to be resolved. Sometimes just airing them is enough, but at others a resolution process is required. Don't let small conflicts fester; they get bigger later on.

B. Hidden Needs Exercise

Purpose: To uncover hidden needs and expectations which may lead to conflicts, to identify what can be done to help a house member meet her/his needs.

Set-up: Each person takes ten minutes of quiet time and writes out answers to the following questions: "How do I normally function in groups?"; "What do I need from the group in order to function at my best?"; "What strengths do I bring to this group?"; "What tensions do I feel with other group members?"; "How can we change our relationship so that we can both grow?" It is not necessary to use all of these questions. Change them as necessary. All of the answers can be recorded on large sheets of paper and posted so that the whole group can read them.

After everyone has spoken, identify the conflicts that have to be resolved and set up times and processes by which community members can begin work on them. Some problems may require that one person simply deal with his/her feelings, others may involve two-person dialogues with a third party, while still others may involve the whole group and require other group meetings to solve problems.

C. Group Meeting with Third Party

Purpose: To identify all the feelings and issues involved in a conflict, to set up a resolution process.

Set-up: 1) Group selects a third party (one or two people).
2) Third party talks individually to each of the people involved and asks: "What are the conflicts as you see them?"; "What are the specific issues?"; "What are the feelings involved?"; "What is your role in the conflict?"; "What can you do to change the situation?"

3) Third party sets up the process for a meeting which allows each member to share their perception of the conflicts; allows everyone to hear each other; provides a time for discussion, and for generation and selection of solutions.
4) Since the third party has talked to each of the people involved he/she may be in the best position to expose the conflicts in the most straightforward manner. "This is what I (we) see going on here... One of the issues that has to be dealt with before the group can move forward is the fact that Jane, while devoting enormous amounts of energy and brilliant thinking to the formation and activities of the group, has effectively blocked others from taking leadership."
5) The third party, either before the meeting or during the sharing and discusison helps sort out the various issues and suggests ways that each of them can be dealt with by the group.
6) Depending on the complexity of the problems and conflicts, a number of meetings may be required to finish the process. Remember—always plan for evaluation both of the agreement and of the process used for reaching agreements.

Each of us has a tremendous store of experience in resolving conflicts of all kinds. We can all learn to draw on that experience to help us find better and better ways to make conflict and its resolution a creative and exciting adventure.

Footnotes:
1. Louis Kriesberg, *The Sociology of Social Conflicts* (Prentice Hall, Englewood Cliffs, N.J., 1973, p. 17).
2. Adam Curle, *Making Peace* (Tavistock, London, G.B., 1971, p.2.).
3. I am indebted to Louis Kriesberg for these categories (see *Sociology of Social Conflicts*).

4. Lewis Coser, *The Functions of Social Conflict* (Free Press, N.Y., N.Y., 1956, p. 61).
5. Kriesberg, p.11.
6. "Who Owns the Problem," a concept from Parent Effectiveness Training (see Thomas Gordon's *Parent Effectiveness Training*).
7. Coser, p. 48-55.
8. Term from George Bach, *The Intimate Enemy* (Avon, New York, N.Y.).
9. Curle, p. 216.
10. Harvey Jackins, *The Human Side of Human Beings*, Rational Island Press.
11. See Gordon above.

Resource Books—Practical
1. George Bach, *Creative Aggression* (Avon, New York, N.Y., 1974).
2. George Bach, *The Intimate Enemy*, (Avon, New York, N.Y., 1974).
3. Thomas Gordon, *Parent Effectiveness Training* (Peter H. Wyden Inc. N.Y., N.Y.)—paperback available also.
4. Coover, Deacon, Esser, & Moore, *Manual for a Living Revolution* (New Society Press, Philadelphia—available through the Movement for a New Society, 4722 Baltimore Ave., Phila., PA 19143).

Resource Books—Theoretical
1. Lewis Coser, *The Functions of Social Conflict* (Free Press, N.Y., N.Y., 1956).
2. Adam Curle, *Making Peace* (Tavistock, London, G.B., 1971).
3. Louis Kriesberg, *The Sociology of Social Conflicts* (Prentice Hall, Englewood Cliffs, N.J., 1973).
4. Gerald Nierenberg, *How to Negotiate* (Cornerstone Library Publications, New York, N.Y., 1975).
5. Paul Wehr, *Conflict Regulation* (American Association for the Advancement of Science, 1776 Mass. Ave., N.W., Washington, D.C. 20036). Note: this is an excellent general work on conflict resolution. I am greatly indebted to Paul for some of the ideas in this paper.

CHAPTER 8
SPINNING THE WEB: NETWORKING AMONG SOCIAL CHANGE ACTIVISTS AND GROUPS

Networks are a somewhat new concept in organizing in the United States. Many of us remember the massive coalitions of the late '60s and '70s. We may also remember working in highly structured organizations with complex hierarchical decision-making procedures, with national office bureaucracies, local chapters, regional offices, etc. Many of us are looking for new ways of working together, having grown tired of the rigidity and complexity of those forms. Networks are seen as an alternative model. But what is a network for social change?

A network is a way to encourage autonomy while providing a means of coordination for the serious struggles that lie before us in our efforts to effect major changes in our society. In a network, each unit has the ability to decide its own direction, in communication and coordination with others.

Those of us working in Movement for a New Society have had some seven years experience in building a network of groups across the United States (and internationally in some ways). But we are still learning and discovering new things about it. Many of the examples and much of the experience reflected in this chapter will be drawn from MNS, but we hope that people will take whatever insights they find here and build their own networks. MNS is used here as an example and something of a model, but there is no presumption that it is possible to organize a network only through MNS.

In this chapter we will look at various types of networks formed for the express purpose of encouraging fundamental social change. In each of these networks the assumption will be that people want to work in egalitarian (i.e.,collective) structures, that groups are seeking ways to connect with other groups in a noncentralist manner, and that there is commitment in the network to nonviolent approaches to change (at least on a tactical, if not ideological/moral basis). Networks can and have been built on other principles, but these are the assumptions in this chapter.

Why Spin the Web?

Why should we encourage the formation of networks? Why not let individuals and groups continue to pursue their projects as they have been? Some of the advantages of acting for change in the context of a network follow. A network:
- Provides a broader outlook, helps us see our personal efforts or those of our group in relation to a larger picture and other efforts being made.
- Counters the feelings that we are in the struggle alone against powerful opposition. Our combined struggles amount to something greater than the sum of the individual efforts.
- Is a way we can give and receive mutual assistance, particularly in times of crisis (what we call "crunch!" times), but also on a regular basis.
- Is a context where we can improve our work for revolutionary change through directed self-study, and mutual appreciation coupled with constructive criticism that pushes us to continually evaluate what we are doing in terms of the task before us.
- Is a base for sharing skills and information.
- Provides a structure through which we can develop common strategies for change in our area/region that will enhance all of our work.
- Can become allied with larger networks—a step that will be necessary if we are to effect the broad changes that are required, most of which will necessitate widespread and coordinated action against powerful forces and institutions in our society. We can't make it alone or in isolation.
- Is a place we can stop our work to have fun, celebrate life in the present moment, make good connnections with others.

Some people may ask how a network is different from a political party. Most parties are run in a centralist, bureaucratic fashion—people gain power and authority by some special characteristic (charisma, seniority) and much of the energy of the party goes into legislative and/or electoral politics. In addition, parties do not encourage local autonomy or the ability of groups to follow their own best judgment. Even the most radical parties often depend on the guidance and directives of experts. Furthermore, most traditional parties do not embrace or nurture the whole person—they are interested in the individual only as a political unit.

I. BEGINNING TO SPIN THE WEB: A NETWORK OF INDIVIDUALS

A network of individuals is a difficult form of social change community to maintain. It is not quite a group with a concrete project or issues that focusses energies. People in it are often involved in individual projects or in other organizations that don't provide them with the kind of support they are looking for. Some people are attracted to a local network of social change people because they are looking for a way to become involved, but don't yet know how they fit it.

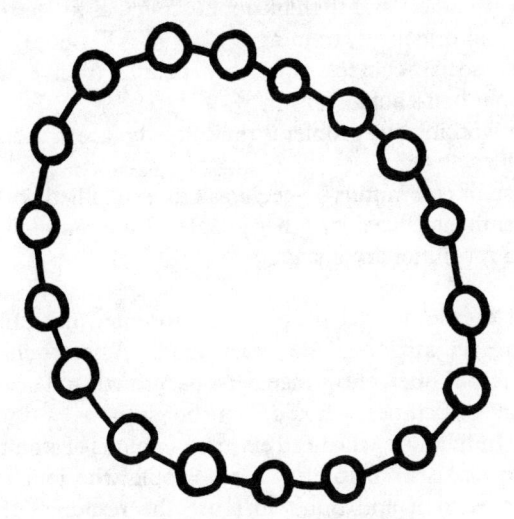

beginning network of individuals

Since the goal of social change networking is to create an effective revolutionary movement, starting networks of individuals is seen as a first step towards that goal. A way must be found to take in new people, to provide them with opportunities for societal analysis and training in organizing skills, and to make them active participants in effective collective efforts. The longer range goal of a network of individuals should be to evolve as people are ready into a system of collective units formed around specific tasks or issues.

No voluntary organization or structure will hold together unless it meets the needs of the people involved. Therefore the first task of people interested in forming a network of individuals is to discover what the common needs are—and then find ways to meet them.

Not all the needs that people bring are identifiable; some will be discovered only after you have worked and struggled together for some time. But some of the more common things that people look for in this form of community are:

- A place to sort out who they are and what they can do in relation to social change.
- Help in pushing themselves to do difficult things in acting for change.
- More information and analysis of society—a way to build a vision with others and to think about strategies for getting there.
- Skills as an organizer, training.
- Friends, social contacts, possibly people to live with in a communal household.
- Help in working out problems they already face in social change work.
- A "sense of community"—feelings close to, allied with, caring about, and challenged by other people with a common commitment to revolutionary change.

Not all of the needs that people bring to a network can be met; people often have inappropriate expectations. A social change network, while it may often encourage personal growth and dealing with psychological difficulties, should not be seen as a therapeutic community. Individuals who need extreme amounts of attention from others would best seek help elsewhere. People who join a network bring resources to it and don't just use the resources they find. Through that kind of balance people feel most empowered, most aware of their own capabilities and potentials.

What Does the Network of Individuals Do?

We have talked about the reasons people join a network, but do their needs get met—concretely?

1) *Study and analysis seminars:* Both newcomers and experienced social change workers have found a need to gather information,

renew their vision of a new society, and devise new ways for achieving our dreams. The "macro-analysis seminar," a self-directed study format designed by MNS, has proven an excellent tool for just this purpose. The seminars have also been a first step for many people toward forming a collective or action project. (The *Macro-Analysis Manual* is available from MNS, 4722 Baltimore Ave., Philadelphia, PA 19143 for $2.40 postpaid).

2) *Strategy Groups:* There is often a need for specific analysis and strategizing about the local area. What are the vital issues in this town, state, region? Who holds the power? What is already being done? Where do we start? Doing such an analysis of your own situation will often lead to starting collectives to work on the issues you have isolated.

3) *Problem-solving for Individuals:* Often people in a network are carrying out lonely struggles within other organizations (human "service" bureaucracies, health systems, industries, more traditional social action agencies, etc.). They need a place where they can think out loud, get ideas for what to do, and get active support for charging ahead.

In Philadelphia there was a small group that met monthly to use a peer-counseling process to think about their social change activities One of the things the group did was to give a block of time at each meeting to one individual in the group. One week Emily talked about her role as a volunteer with Women Organized Against Rape and problems that were coming up for her. Others in the group that questioned her made suggestions, and asked Emily what kinds of help she needed to act on some of the better suggestions. People in a network can learn problem-solving techniques and give individual attention to each other. It is often enough just to let a person think out loud and get some feedback without using any fancy techniques.

4) *Training:* A network of individuals can organize training weekends for themselves through which they can gain more skills, confidence, and clarity in order to become more active and effective in change efforts. For instance, in the spring of 1976, a series of workshops was held for people (mostly familiar with MNS) in New England. First there was an open workshop on conflict resolution. Later, a smaller group of people who had had more training experiences and who were interested in becoming trainers themselves came together for a four-day "training for trainers" session. For

both of these workshops trainers came from Philadelphia. At the end of the second weekend the trainers travelled with workshop participants to their home situations and worked with groups they were members of in providing help on group process skills and resolving some conflicts as well. Large numbers of participants in these workshops helped provide a solid base for the work of the Clamshell Alliance against the nuclear power plant in Seabrook, New Hampshire.

5) *Clearness Meetings:* Most of us get three kinds of feedback from other people: putdowns, advice, or pleasant positive feedback that doesn't really take into account who we are or the needs of the situation. "Clearness" meetings provide a way for people to be thought about in depth—to receive both positive and negative feedback. Clearness is a valuable way of nurturing people who are in transition, who are looking for new directions, or who are new to the process of social change work.

6) *Individual Crunch:* Families or individuals within a social change network may have crises in relation to social change work or some personal matter. If people in the network can respond, it will build the bonds and strengthen the commitment people feel toward each other.

7) *Workdays:* Within a network of individuals you can set aside a day to help one person or a group with a project. Collating parties that combine drudge work with socializing have become a tradition with some groups. In rural areas the possibilities are unlimited, but even in the city people's houses can use good work that friends can join in on.

8) *Working on Feelings:* One of the aims of a network of social change activists is encouraging people (both individuals and whole segments of society) to (re)discover their innate power, creativity, and human-ness. To become empowered in this way, we have to deal with all the feelings that are the opposite of that: powerlessness, hopelessness, self put-downs. In the past ten years the human potential movement has developed a number of techniques for doing that. The one we have found to be most successful and conforming most closely to principles of personal empowerment (i.e., nondependence on professionals or experts) is Re-evaluation Counseling (also called "co-counseling"), a peer counseling method where people learn the skills for helping each other deal with feelings

on an "equal time" basis. There is no contradiction between personal growth and political work—they both need our attention on our way to a new society.

9) *Share Ourselves:* A network of individuals can set aside time, either as a whole group or in smaller groups, to get to know one another better. One thing that has proven a powerful experience is to hear peoples' personal histories—where they have come from, the struggles they have seen, and their joys. Time needs to be taken to hear from each person. Brief time for sharing can be made a regular part of meetings.

10) *Fun and Celebration!!!:* We can give attention and vent to the joy within us and celebrate each other—not forgetting the serious nature of our work, but reminding ourselves constantly of the ways we enjoy each other and life around us. We can also set aside special times to celebrate—particular occasions when we can play, sing, engage in sports, and eat good food.

II. THE WEB EVOLVES: AFFINITY GROUPS AND COLLECTIVES EMERGE

Affinity Groups

Even a network of fifteen or twenty would do well to form three or four smaller groups to provide ongoing support for its members. In MNS we have often used the term "affinity group" to refer to the ongoing small group where people engage in study, support for personal growth, and social change work. Such a group is small enough for people in it to get to know each other well. Affinity groups can also take on a task or issue focus if they choose. The group that wrote this book, the Training/Action Affinity Group, has been an active training team for several years. While we engage in much work together, an important part of our collective life is the attention we give to each others' personal growth.

The folks who are interested in forming an affinity group can agree how often they want to meet with each other, what kinds of things they want to do with that time, and what their expectations of each other are. As sub-groups form within the network, all of the activities described above in the section on a network of individuals can continue, but many of them will now be carried out in the smaller groupings. There will continue to be a need, however, for gatherings of the whole network and some way to coordinate activities, welcome and include new people, etc. Responsibility for making sure that these things happen can be rotated among the groups in the network.

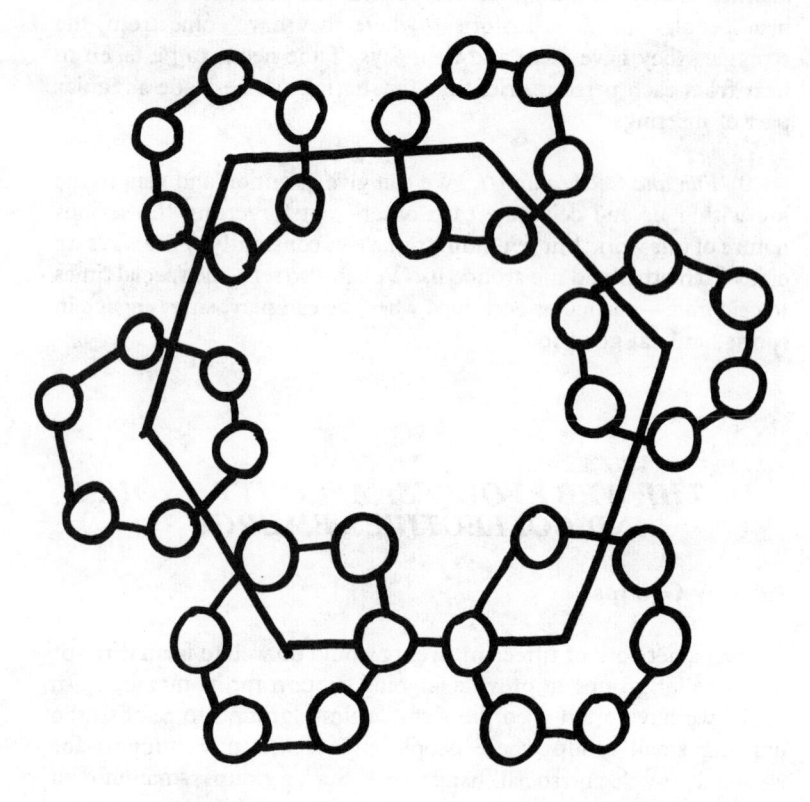

Network of individuals in affinity groups

Collectives

As the affinity groups do their work and the network grows, people begin to coalesce around common interests or tasks that need to get done. Such groups can become collectives. There are a number of different kinds of collectives—each has a structure implied by the task to be performed, but no two collectives function alike.

SPINNING THE WEB: NETWORKS FOR SOCIAL CHANGE

The basic kinds of collectives are:

1) *Issue/Campaign Collectives*—these are formed to work on specific issues such as health care, peace conversion, workplace organizing, nuclear power, etc.

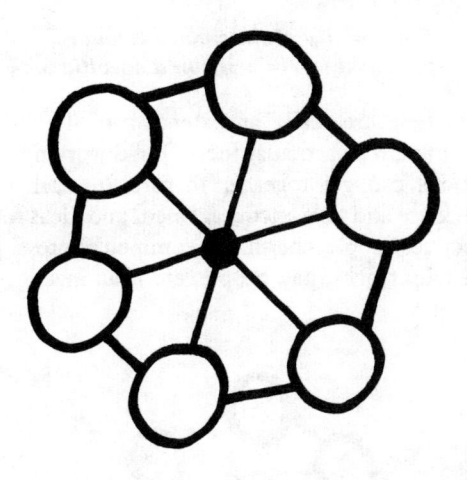

campaign, organizing collective or alternative institution; there can be a dual focus—on a specific task and on support for individuals

2) *Alternative Institutions*—these are established to provide a service in a new way. Examples include food coops, collective print shops, recycling systems, cooperative daycare centers, etc.

3) *Organizing Collectives*—these take on a particular kind of organizing task such as training programs, starting study seminars, literature sales and correspondence, orienting new people, etc.

4) *Community Maintenance Groups*—these take on tasks which relate to the common life of the network. For instance, there might be a group set up with representatives from each collective that talks about common strategy ideas, or provides orientation sessions for interested people.

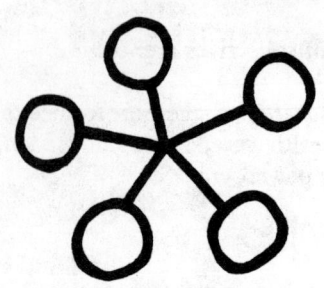

Community Maintenance Group:
usually the group focusses primarily on a specific task to be done

5) *Caucuses*—these are really an extension of the affinity group concept, but with a particular focus. Folks working within other organizations can get together to listen to each other about that experience and give encouragement and ideas for how to be most effective. People who share a common oppression (women, young people, blacks, gay people, etc.) can meet to share their struggles.

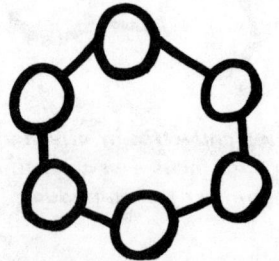

affinity group or caucus; the main focus
is on support of individuals

When collectives first begin to form there may be only a few of them and communication will be fairly easy. The network is still an informal organization. Coordination and common strategy are not needed yet. In the next section we will look at what happens as the network of groups expands and becomes more complex.

III. THE NETWORK EXPANDS: A MORE FORMAL NETWORK OF GROUPS

This section will explore the advantages of forming a closely knit network of groups and discuss some of the functions of such a local network. We are talking here about an alliance of collectives, caucuses, affinity groups, alternative institutions, etc. into one organization, but maintaining each unit's ability to choose its own directions. Such a network involves communication and information sharing among constituent elements.

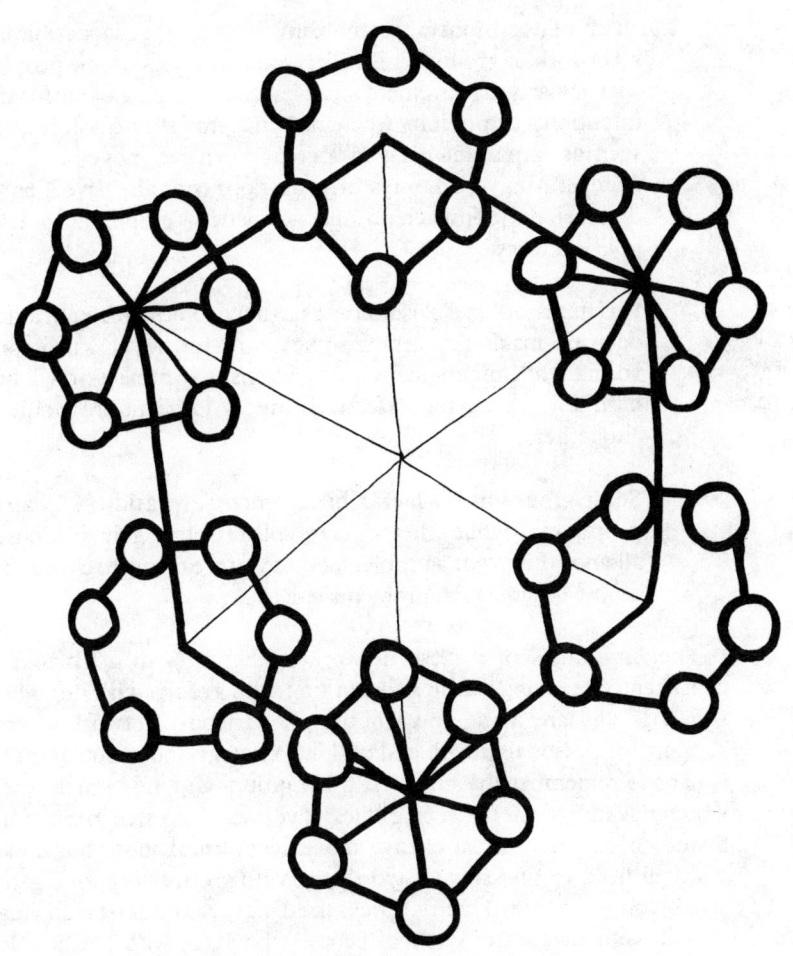

Loose network of affinity groups and collectives

Why Build Your Own Network?

What are the advantages of building your own network of groups rather than attempting to pull together existing groups into a network?

1) It enables you to have a more cohesive organization with common philosophy, organizational style, and strategy for change.

2) Many of us are looking for more involvement than is possible in a network of groups with widely varying styles. Some people (particularly in Movement for a New Society) are looking for an intentional community where personal growth and politics are seen as important parts of a comprehensive movement for change. Many traditional organizations (not all) have a uni-dimensional approach to change, usually emphasizing the political work.

3) It is necessary in a close network to have some agreement as to decision-making process. If some groups in a network insist on voting while others insist on a consensus approach, it will be hard to work together effectively unless decisions are avoided altogether.

4) Some groups have a hierarchical structure (presidents, chair-people, etc.) while others operate collectively. Again, in a loose alliance this is not a problem, but if you are trying to coexist in a close organization problems will erupt.

The limitations of a close network is that it is difficult to be consistently reaching out to and working with groups with different styles. If you are living and working in a friendly network where support for personal growth and political strategy and action exist, it is hard to remember that there are other groups and individuals with whom it is important to become allies. If you are interested in creating a well-coordinated social change movement throughout your area, you will need to find some way to work with groups with divergent styles from your own. There is always the danger of huddling—staying only in your nice warm circle of people who agree with you and do things your way and thus avoiding moving out into the world where things are a bit scary. In a later section, we will talk about the formation of networks with other groups and organizations with different styles and principles.

Operating Your Network

But how, concretely, does the close network we are talking about here operate? We will assume that many of the activities described in the section on networks of individuals are continuing. Some of the particular activities of the local network of collectives are:

1) *Communications*—Collectives will need to share regularly with each other about their programs and actions to get a sense of the thrust and impact of the whole network. This can be done as quick reports at a network meeting or through an informal newsletter.

2) *Ongoing Vision, Strategy, Analysis*—Each collective continues to review its own analysis of the present situation, vision for the future, and strategy for getting there. It may be important to hold strategy sessions which include people from each collective to evaluate the effectiveness of the social change work of the whole network, in order to gain coherence and a sense of the whole and which will allow each collective to set its own course in that light.

3) *Collective Clearness*—In MNS we have had considerable experience using the clearness process in relation to groups— both at the point of their joining the network for periodic review of their work and strategy. It is wise to call a special meeting to which members of several collectives are asked to come, forming a "clearness committee." Such a clearness meeting might focus on the following issues:

- The analysis of the collective in regard to their particular issue or work, including how it connects with other issues or efforts.

- Their vision for that issue and strategy for getting there— how the work they are doing right now fits into that strategy and into the work of other collectives and overall network strategy.

- Plans and possibilities for the collective for the next year.

- Positive feedback and constructive criticism from members of the clearness committee.

In the fall of 1976, members of several MNS collectives in Philadelphia met to have a clearness meeting for two collectives with related activities. By the end of the meetings, both collectives were disbanded and a new group was formed combining the functions of the former group.

4) *Network Meetings*—Getting the network together for both fun and business is a good idea. Sometimes, meetings are all business (reports, discussions, decision-making), but often a large chunk of time is set aside to focus on the work of one collective or to have some special presentation of general interest.

5) *Crunch*—Collectives in the network can respond to requests from other collectives for help during times of crises (particularly crucial points of a direct action campaign, for aid with financial difficulties, or for assistance in resolving internal conflicts). For instance, within the Philadelphia MNS Network, the Community Associates Printing Collective was plagued by continual financial problems and internal personality conflicts. Over a period of a year or more they were assisted by numerous individuals and collectives from the network and finally helped in making the decision to close the shop and sell the equipment to help defray the debt.

If your local network is part of a larger network, *crunch* calls may come from far away collectives. During the Native American occupation of Wounded Knee in South Dakota, an MNS collective in the Midwest called *crunch* and received assistance from MNS people in Philadelphia, Oregon and Wisconsin who came to help form a nonviolent interventionary force between the occupiers of the American Indian Movement and federal authorities.

6) We have already mentioned the need to build enjoyable time into all of the work you do, but the whole network can also take days off to play and relax together, pay attention to the environment and each other, and thereby avoid the "burnout" syndrome that has plagued overcommitted radicals for years.

Joining the Network

Such networks as we have been talking about in this section need to develop some process for accepting new collectives. Since there are expectations and responsibilities of groups in the network, it is best to know who is "in" and who is "out." In MNS we use the clearness process whereby representatives of two or more collectives in the network meet with the collective that wishes to join the network. Together they come to mutual decision on whether the new group should join. If everyone agrees then someone from the "old" collective writes a letter to the MNS internal newsletter as does someone from the "new" collective—informing everyone else in the network about the work of the newcomer. If the representatives from the old collectives do not agree then the new group can bring its request to the next network meeting.

The criteria used for a collective to join the network are as follows:

1) General acceptance of the analysis and vision which MNS has evolved thus far; commitment to a nonviolent revolutionary strategy; and involvement in continued study and learning-through-action to further develop theory shared among MNS groups.

2) The group is actively working to bring about a new society and understands the place of its work in a long-term revolutionary strategy consistent with theory shared among MNS groups.

3) The group has a democratic structure and process and is willing to strive with the rest of the MNS network in making our personal lives and political beliefs consistent.

4) Commitment to work both individually and collectively to rid themselves of our internalized racism, sexism, classism, heterosexism, and ageism.

5) Willingness to participate fully in the MNS network. This includes taking part in network decisions, communicating with the rest of the network, readiness to offer and receive

criticism, and commitment to provide mutual aid and respond to *crunch*.

6) The group is willing to use consensus decision making at network meetings.

EXTENDING THE WEB: REGIONAL AND ISSUE-ORIENTED NETWORKS

As we said earlier, it is important to avoid the phenomenon of "huddling" (sticking with the people and groups that feel comfortable and safe) and actively strive to work with groups which may have somewhat different principles and organizational styles than our own. If we are to win skirmishes with powerful institutions and move on to substantial victories, we must take on the building of a more cohesive movement. The competition and debilitating ideological wrangles which have immobilized the Left in the past must be eliminated. We have neither the time nor the energy to spend cutting each other down, but should look for ways to encourage each other, lend assistance when needed, and give forthright constructive criticism when appropriate.

There are several different kinds of alliances that can be built between social change groups of different flavors:

- Local or regional networks of social change groups of all styles, ideologies, and issues—"potpourri networks."

- Local or regional networks of social change groups working on the same issue.

- National (or transnational) networks that provide a broader base of mutual support and the capability of greater pressure on the institutions we seek to change.

SPINNING THE WEB: NETWORKS FOR SOCIAL CHANGE

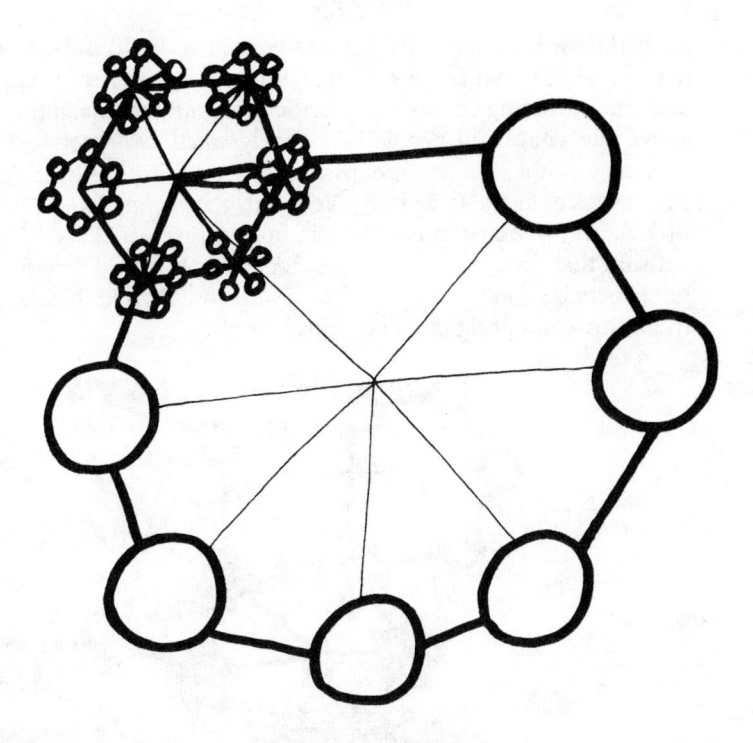

Potpourri network: a loose network of area social change groups

Potpourri Networks

A network which draws into alliance all groups committed to basic change throughout the area can be quite effective, so long as they do not get bogged down in pointless debates over style or ideology. The point is not to create a new organization to which all the constituent groups become members (such as the close network of collectives described in the previous section), but to provide a channel of communication and cooperation that makes each group's efforts more effective. Therefore, such a network can remain somewhat loose and informal, concentrating on building personal connections between people and sharing information and resources.

People sometimes wonder which kind of network to organize. The answer will depend on the type of area you are working in, the kinds of groups that are working there, the issues that are vital to the area, and the energies you or your group have. However, "potpourri networks" will probably be more important to build in rural areas than in large urban centers. Usually in rural areas there is at most one group working on any one specific issue and the total number of active and concerned people is relatively small. So a network that embraces all the different groups and issues is fairly easily achieved. For instance, in St. Johnsbury, Vermont, there is perhaps a core of fifty radical or "alternative" people in a county of 22,000. A local network that brings all those people together periodically might well be beneficial (and could capitalize on the myriad overlapping friendships and group memberships!).

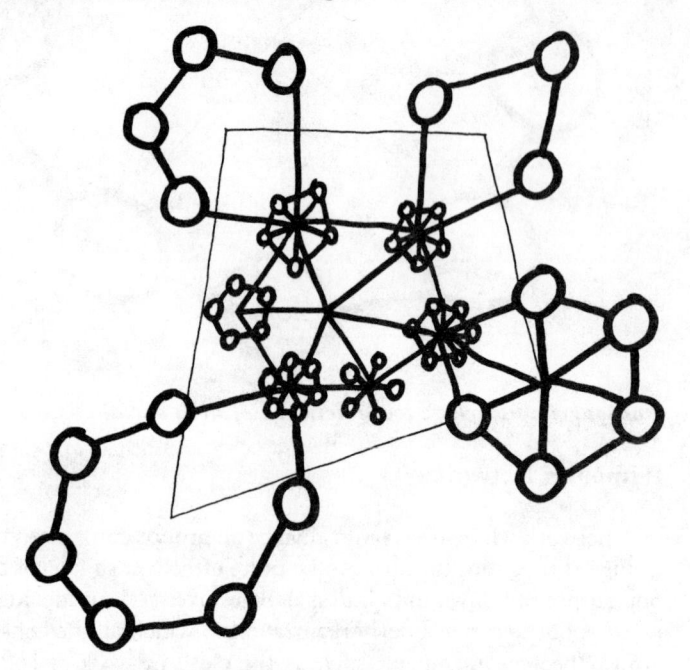

Issue-oriented networks with tentative ties between them

Issue Networks

Most of us have seen issue networks at one time or another in the past. Many of the coalitions of the 1960's were actually large networks of people concerned about the war in Vietnam. But most of those coalitions were formed in a time of crisis for a limited purpose— and most dissolved as soon as the immediate project or mass rally passed. We hope that the kind of network we are talking about will prove longer-lived and of more mutual benefit. We are already seeing all across the country extensive networks of feminist groups forming—often around such issues as health care for women or getting the Equal Rights Amendment passed.

An excellent example of a network formed around an issue of vital interest is the Clamshell Alliance in New Hampshire and its extensive ramifications throughout New England. It is a multilevel network beginning with groups in the immediate area opposing the Seabrook nuclear power plant. The Clamshell Alliance has strong connections with environmental and alternative energy groups throughout New England. There are also bonds with national organizations who can work at the national level in Washington against the Seabrook plant and against nuclear power in general. For their large actions, the Clamshell Alliance puts a call out for help from all environmental and social change groups and activists within reasonable distance to come to Seabrook and join in.

For people organizing in cities it may be easier to begin to work on issue networks rather than the "potpourri" type—just because there are often so many groups working for change in large urban areas. Eventually ties can be built between the different issue networks— thus a network of women's centers could respond to a *crunch* call by a prison abolition network (or provide special resources, or cooperate on a project concerning women in prisons, etc.).

It should be acknowledged that many of these kinds of networks exist already, although they are ad hoc and informal and there has been no explicit agreement as to what groups in them can expect from each other. Many of the informal and unacknowledged networks are working well; many others would benefit from a more intentional approach with clear agreements.

We have found that what really holds a network together is personal contacts and friendships. Local, state or regional networks are built best by individuals making visits to people in other places, taking the time to establish friendships before jumping into meetings where there are a lot of people who have never seen each other before. Even when it is time for a big gathering it pays to set aside relaxed time for people to get to know one another and not fill every moment with pressing business.

In building either a potpourri or issue network there are some general principles that can be mentioned about how they can be formed and how they can function:

- Individual contacts and personal visits help bind a network.

- Start informally with regular sharing of information and resources, and semi-social events where people can get to know each other and discover common interests.

- Adopt common strategies and coordinated efforts around *specific* vital struggles.

- Work towards more *general* and *regular* cooperation, coordination and common strategy.

- Develop a *crunch* response system.

- Encourage mutual appreciation and constructive criticism.

- Celebrate each other and the good work happening.

V. THE WIDER WEB: NATIONAL AND TRANSNATIONAL NETWORKS

MNS has been a national network since its beginning (1971), with groups starting in Wisconsin, Oregon and Pennsylvania almost simultaneously. In recent years since then regional networks have emerged as more groups were formed (Northeast, Mid-Atlantic, Southeast, Midwest, Northwest, Southwest, etc.) Regions have met when they wanted to—usually about every six months. A National Network meeting is held once a year and friendships formed during that weeklong event last and grow during the year and are nurtured by lots of intervisiting across the country. A newsletter called the *WINE* brings us news and ideas from throughout the network. MNS has at the same time established contacts with groups and individuals involved with social change in Canada, Europe, Japan, New Zealand, India, Australia, Thailand, and Bangladesh.

We have found the experience of this kind of wider network to be important and enjoyable. It keeps us in touch with people in many places and allows us to benefit from their experience and they from ours. In times of crisis it is good to know that we can call upon people from the other side of the country if need be. For international campaigns (such as one that dealt with apartheid and exploitation in Namibia), we can call upon cooperation from friends in Europe and elsewhere for a many-fronted effort.

Networks are still a relatively new concept. We all have a lot to learn. We hope that you will take ideas from this chapter and adapt them to your own situation, invent new systems for yourselves, and then share that experience with other people who are struggling with similar efforts to make this a better world. Each time we reach out to build bonds with each other it brings us closer to that vision. Happy Networking!

RESOURCES AVAILABLE
FROM MOVEMENT FOR A NEW SOCIETY
(all items postpaid; prices subject to change)

Moving Toward a New Society. Gowan, Lakey, Moyer, and Taylor. Analysis, vision, and strategy for a democratic, decentralized, and ecologically sound new society. $5.50

Resource Manual for a Living Revolution, alias "The Monster Manual." Coover, Deacon, Esser, and Moore. Skills and resources for organizing for fundamental social change from a nonviolent perspective. $5.70

Strategy for a Living Revolution. Lakey. Historically based five-stage strategic model. $7.50

A Manifesto for Nonviolent Revolution. Lakey. Original working draft outlining analysis, vision, and strategy for the MNS network. $1.15

New Society Packet. Includes papers on analysis, vision, struggle, training, alternative institutions, community lifestyles, and the network; and a bibliography. $.70

On Organizing Macro-Analysis Seminars. Philadelphia Macro-Analysis Collective. A do-it-yourself manual for local groups to study their political/economic environment and to act upon it. Includes updated reading list. $2.40

An MNS Feminist Bibliography. Mallory. $1.15

Dedeveloping the U.S. Through Nonviolence. Moyer. Good on strategy. $.45

Working Toward a New Society and a Critique of American Marxism. Albert. "What is to be done?" from a nonviolent perspective. $1.75

Blockade! Taylor. Story of MNS's successful blockade of U.S. arms to Pakistan in 1971. Includes nonviolent action manual. $3.45

Theory of Sexism. Bedard and Castle. Analysis of male domination; visions of a new non-patriarchal society. $.150

Off Their Backs and On Our Own Two Feet. Men against patriarchy. Men's writing on liberation from sexism. $1.75

Gay Oppression and Liberation, or "Homophobia: Its Causes and Cure." $3.50

No More Plastic Jesus: Global Justice and Christian Lifestyle. Finnerty. Analysis of global social/economic situation, vision and strategy for a just world from a Christian perspective. $4.45

A Nonviolent Action Manual. Moyer. Step-by-step procedures for organizing demonstrations, campaigns. $1.75

Clearness: Processes for Supporting Individuals and Groups in Decision-Making. Woodrow. $1.75

Taking Charge. Simple Living Collective. Practical suggestions for change in our daily lives and communities. $2.75

Dandelion. MNS quarterly newsletter. $3.50/year.

To order literature, for a complete literature list, or for some more information about MNS and contacts in your area, write:

In the Northeast,
MOVEMENT FOR A NEW SOCIETY
4722 Baltimore Avenue
Philadelphia, Pennsylvania 19143

In the Southeast,
ATLANTA MNS
Post Office Box 5434
Atlanta, Georgia 30307